# In Defence of the Realm?

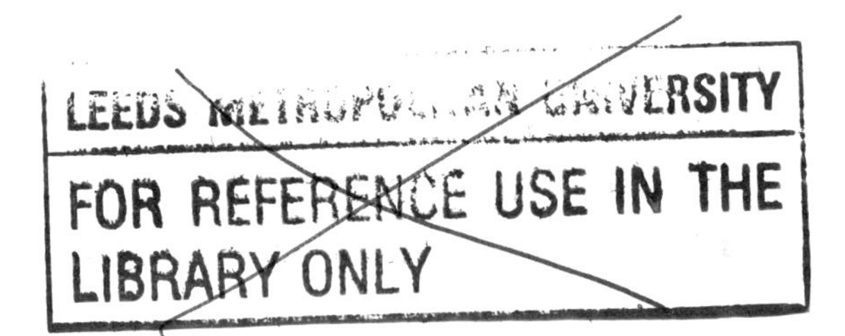

# In Defence of the Realm?

## The Case for Accountable Security Services

by

Richard Norton-Taylor

The Civil Liberties Trust

The Civil Liberties Trust
21 Tabard Street
London SE1 4LA



**British Library Cataloguing In Publication Data**

Norton-Taylor, Richard
In Defence of the Realm?: The Case for Accountable
Security Services
1. British Intelligence Services
1. Title
327.1′2′0941

ISBN 0-900137-31-2

The Trust's publications do not necessarily reflect the views of the Trust.



Designed by Jeff Sanders, Edward Bear Associates, London.
Typeset in Stempel Garamond and ITC Garamond.
Printed by Crowes, Norwich.

# Acknowledgments

This book was conceived by the Civil Liberties Trust back in 1988 when the Government, it seemed, was turning a blind eye to increasing public concern about the activities of the security services - in particular, MI5 - and the absence of any statutory guidelines setting out their role in law.

Whitehall, however, was not idle. Prompted partly by this growing public concern, but also by two cases involving MI5 taken by the National Council for Civil Liberties (*Liberty*) to the European Commission of Human Rights, it drew up a Security Service Bill. The Bill was announced in the Queen's Speech in November 1988 and became law a year later.

But while this new Act gives no role to Parliament to oversee the activities of Britain's security and intelligence agencies, parallel legislation - the new Official Secrets Act which came into force on 1 March 1990 - places further obstacles in the way of finding out what the agencies are up to.

I am grateful, however, that the Government has continued the debate, albeit perhaps unintentionally. The measures which it hoped would put an end to discussion about the security and intelligence services have done nothing of the kind. I am especially grateful to *Liberty* for helping to hold up the flickering candle of civil liberties despite a depressing lack of enthusiasm from Parliament or the public at large.

My first personal thanks are to Sara Huey, former Director of the Civil Liberties Trust, who commissioned this book and devoted much of her time to the project - as did all the others mentioned below. I would like to thank those who read and made comments on drafts. They include Tony Bunyan, Alf Dubbs and Malcolm Hurwitt. Madeleine Colvin, *Liberty*'s Legal Officer, and Renée Harris, *Liberty*'s Publications Officer, provided especially valuable advice. Thanks also to Marie Ryan for typing numerous amendments to the final draft. I am indebted above all to Patricia Tillin of *Liberty*, whose cheerfulness and technological skills supported me to the end, and Francesca Klug, current Director of the Civil Liberties Trust, whose tolerance and patience were as remarkable as her editing skills. Without them, this book would not have seen the light of day.

*Richard Norton-Taylor, March 1990.*

The Civil Liberties Trust would like to acknowledge the contribution towards production costs made by a small trust fund. This trust, which wishes to remain anonymous, derives from an inheritance which was renounced and deposited tax-free with the Charities Aid Foundation.

## About the Author

Since 1976 Richard Norton-Taylor has reported on Whitehall, including security matters, for *The Guardian* newspaper. Prior to this he covered the European Community and NATO from Brussels. Previous publications include *Blacklist* (with Mark Hollingsworth, Hogarth, Press 1988) and *The Ponting Affair* (Cecil Woolf, 1984).

## About the Civil Liberties Trust

The Civil Liberties Trust, sister organisation to the National Council for Civil Liberties, is an educational charity which was founded in 1963 to provide research and information on civil liberty issues.

# Contents

# INTRODUCTION

Britain's security and intelligence services are at a watershed. Their senior officers know they are fighting a losing battle against an overwhelming, though rarely articulated, belief that they should be held to account to an independent body and drop the faded curtain of secrecy surrounding them.

During the summer of 1989, Patrick Walker, Director-General of the Security Service (MI5), made it clear in a series of discreet meetings in Whitehall that he had come round to the view – already shared by his predecessor, Sir Antony Duff, and most of his staff – that something must be done to improve the agency's public image, battered by a series of scandals about its past activities. Those scandals and controversies – ranging from MI5's past activities in Northern Ireland to the vetting of ministers and targeting of innocent individuals – fed latent suspicion and distrust about the present role of MI5, the police Special Branch (MI5's footsoldiers) and the rest of the intelligence establishment.

Questions about their role and targets may be the last thing the security and intelligence services want, especially in the context of their fight against violent terrorism. But past experience has not earned them the right to automatic trust. Even their counterparts within NATO are urging the security and intelligence services to be more open, whilst in the context of recent, momentous changes their traditional rivals in Eastern Europe are presenting themselves to public scrutiny. Against this background, Mr Walker, whose appointment early in 1988 was itself an official secret, was wondering barely a year later whether the time was ripe for him to come out of the Whitehall closet and show himself to MPs, the press and the public.

The idea of holding up security and intelligence agencies to independent oversight is not new to the unelected officials who take responsibility for guarding our national security. Over ten years ago, during the aftermath of the Watergate scandal in the US and at a time when West Germany opened up its intelligence services to parliamentary scrutiny, top Whitehall officials met in secret to discuss the possible implications for Britain. Would Britain, they wondered anxiously, be forced to go down the same road? There is no record of their meetings; indeed, ministers did not even know the discussions had taken place.[1]

The latest discreet manoeuvrings in the summer of 1989 had the sniff of a classic Whitehall ploy: agree to limited reforms to avoid pressure for more radical ones and trim the sails of those, including MPs from all parties, wanting more. This book argues the case for reforms that will place the security and intelligence agencies under democratic scrutiny. It sets out the debate about the role and status of the security and intelligence agencies in the light of the scandals that have plagued them and the myths that surround them. It does so against the background of a new Official Secrets Act which, if ministers have their way, will smother that debate.

It challenges the 'we know best, trust us' attitude adopted by successive British governments and makes detailed recommendations about how to subject Britain's security and intelligence agencies to independent accountability without jeopardising the nation's security. It is a challenge which British governments, in contrast with their closest allies, have persistently refused to meet. Britain is alone among the major liberal democracies in having no system of independent oversight to hold to account the activities of these agencies and in refusing to allow Parliament behind what the Government calls the 'barriers of secrecy'.[2]

Successive governments have perpetuated an aura of mystery around the security and intelligence agencies. It is time for discussion and treatment of them – so often hovering between the realms of fact and fiction, the exotic and the seedy – to be brought down to earth. For in reality they are the last refuge for those in Whitehall who want to continue to enjoy power without responsibility. As the historian, Christopher Andrew, has put it, they are the 'last taboo' of British politics.[3] Yet they suffer from the same ambitions and frailties and fall to the same temptations as any other part of the state bureaucracy. Only in their case, conspiracies and distortions flourish in a secret and unaccountable world, compounding the dangers to our civil liberties.

We will look at the record and the activities of Britain's four main security and intelligence services. They are the Security Service or MI5, which is responsible for counter-espionage, counter–terrorism, and counter–'subversion' in Britain and the colonies; the Special Branch (SB); the Secret Intelligence Service or MI6, which runs agents and collects intelligence by covert means abroad (and which officially does not exist in peacetime); and the Government Communications Headquarters (GCHQ), the electronic intelligence–gathering agency whose budget and manpower greatly exceed those of MI5 and MI6 combined.

We will look, too, at their structures, operations and targets and show how the kinds of scandals and mistakes that have dogged Britain's security services have led other western democracies such as Canada and Australia to introduce independent scrutiny and controls. We shall consider the arguments for and against accountability, including the evidence that, contrary to what British governments have claimed, secrecy does not promote efficiency. Often, quite the reverse has proved true.

The security and intelligence agencies, armed with increasingly intrusive technology and developing more and more ties with the private sector, have formed a kind of intelligence/industrial complex which enjoys unique privileges. It is true they have a special and valuable role, combating violent terrorism, sabotage and espionage. But their activities are not restricted to these accepted targets. Often, they can affect the ordinary, innocent, citizen. As one former MI5 officer, Miranda Ingram, has put it: '[MI5's] vetting assessment may ruin somebody's career'.[4]

# CHAPTER ONE

# Induction to a Closed World

'Ordinary people', Prime Minister Margaret Thatcher said at the height of the *Spycatcher* affair, 'are much more in touch with security matters than people in the media.' This statement was part of a concerted government attempt to brush aside increasingly widespread concern, going well beyond the allegations in ex-MI5 officer Peter Wright's memoirs,[1] about the security and intelligence services. The message was simple: we should not bother ourselves with such matters. Successive ministers have tried to shrug off the debate by saying that as far as their constituents are concerned, it is a non-issue.

## Whose security?

The Government wants us to believe that it is only the 'chattering classes' who are concerned about the activities of the security services. It wants us to believe that these agencies are concerned only with threats from violent terrorists, notably the IRA, and with guarding our secrets from foreign spies. These are among their priorities. But they are just a part of the concerns of these unaccountable agencies of the state. The tentacles of the security services reach much further. They can intrude into every household in the country. They can listen in on any telephone conversation. The methods they employ and the operations they undertake are secret. There is no right to know in Britain – no Freedom of Information Act and, on the other side of the same coin – no Privacy Act. There is no way of knowing whether the extraordinary amount of information held on individuals by the security and intelligence agencies is accurate or how much is based on hearsay or whim.

The debate about the role of these agencies is intimately bound up with the whole question of official secrecy and the relationship between an increasingly weak Parliament and an increasingly powerful executive.

It also concerns another fundamental, but far from philosophical, question: whether the state represents the public interest – all of its citizens – or is simply a synonym for the government of the day.

The judge in the 1985 official secrets trial of former Ministry of Defence civil servant, Clive Ponting, had no hesitation in identifying the state with the Government. Mr Justice McCowan told the jury that 'the policies of the state were the policies of the Government then in power'.[2] The Attorney-General at the time, Sir Michael Havers, told the Commons that the Government agreed with that statement as a matter of law. A similar proposition – that the interests of the state are what the government of the day says they are – was accepted by 441 votes to 94 in the German Reichstag on March 23, 1933. It was called the Enabling Law and made Adolf Hitler the sole arbiter of Germany's national interest.

Shortly after her suggestion that the public – if not the courts – was right behind the Government in its failed attempt to ban *Spycatcher* in Britain, Margaret Thatcher told the Conservative backbench MP, Richard Shepherd, that his attempt early in 1988 to reform the Official Secrets Act involved issues which went 'to the heart of government'. It was for the Government, and the Government alone, she implied, to dictate the content of new secrets legislation. 'Our proposals,' she said, 'must reflect the view we take, as the government of the day, on what is necessary in the national interest.'[3] On her instructions Mr Shepherd's Bill was killed in the Commons by a three-line government whip.

She had let the cat out of the bag: as far as information about the security services – indeed, information held by any employees of the state – is concerned, it is for the government, and the government alone, to decide what to disclose. The assertion that the public, or national, interest is identical to the government's is reflected throughout the new Official Secrets Act. Repeated attempts to introduce a 'public interest defence' to allow officials and editors to claim in court that they disclosed information to reveal illegal acts, for example, or abuse of authority, were rejected by Home Office ministers.

The 1989 Official Secrets Act imposes an absolute, life-long, duty of silence on members and former members of the security and intelligence services. The Security Service Act – which was also pushed through the Commons at the same time, early in 1989 – gives the Home Secretary unlimited and unaccountable discretion in his use of MI5. The Government dismissed every meaningful amendment to these two pieces of legislation – legislation with serious constitutional implications – tabled by MPs from all parties, including former Conservative cabinet ministers. The implication was clear: Parliament, let alone the public, has no right to know what Whitehall in general – and the security and intelligence agencies in particular – are up to.

Moreover MI5's functions, as spelt out in the Security Service Act, give the agency a wide measure of discretion. The same holds true for the police Special Branch guidelines.[4] Just how widely they have been interpreted was demonstrated by Merlyn Rees, the former Labour Home Secretary. 'The Special Branch', he told the Commons on March 2, 1978, 'collects information on those whom I think cause problems for the State.'[5] In theory, the agencies are accountable to ministers; the practice, however, is very different. Rees himself has acknowledged that he was not aware of what the security services were up to when he was in government as Home Secretary and Northern Ireland Secretary.

## The origins of the security and intelligence services

The early history of the security and intelligence services, let alone their later operations, has never been placed on official record. Perhaps it is not surprising given the haphazard, and at times almost farcical, stages of their development.

The circumstances of their origin were not auspicious. In 1909, at a time of anti-German xenophobia, the Cabinet set up a group of officials under the Committee of Imperial Defence to consider what the Government had convinced itself was a growing threat of foreign espionage. A Secret Service Bureau was established and was divided in 1910 into two departments: one responsible for counter-espionage at home, later to become the Security Service or MI5; the other in charge of intelligence-gathering overseas, the future Secret Intelligence Service, or MI6.

The spy mania of the time – encouraged by an unscrupulous thriller-writer, William le Queux, who fed on public fantasies and found it difficult to distinguish between fact and fiction – coupled with the genuine threat of imminent war with Germany, also led to the 1911 Official Secrets Act.[6] The Act sped through the Commons in one hot afternoon in August. Its wording was so broad it covered not only espionage but, despite the denial of ministers, the disclosure and receipt of any official information. The Act, which became so discredited that the Government could no longer be confident of securing jury convictions under it, was finally replaced in 1989. While removing the disclosure of official information about most domestic issues from the criminal law, the new Act covers all information concerning security and intelligence, defence, and international relations. Section 1 of the 1911 Act, however, which deals with espionage, remains in force.

The 1911 Act was followed by a further Official Secrets Act in 1920. This introduced new sanctions against entering military establishments fraudulently and enabled the government to obtain warrants to order private cable and postal companies to hand over material to the government. This Act is still in force and could have increasing relevance in the light of the privatisation of British Telecom. A further Official Secrets Act in 1939 amended Section 6 of the 1920 Act by stating that it was the duty of a citizen to reveal the sources of his or her information in relation to matters covered by Section 1 of the 1911 Act. This Act is also still in force.

The essentially military origins of the Security Service and Secret Intelligence Service are betrayed by their common, shorthand, names: MI5 and MI6 – MI for Military Intelligence – titles which also serve to disguise their true role. Although they are responsible to the Home Office, MI5 officers still describe themselves as Ministry of Defence employees or researchers.

The Special Branch (SB) grew out of the Metropolitan Police (the Met) Special Irish Branch set up in 1883 to counter the activities of the Irish

Republican Brotherhood, the successor to the Fenians. Initially the Special Branch was run entirely by the Metropolitan Police and the great majority of its officers were based in London.

The Government Communications Headquarters (GCHQ) developed from the Government Code & Cypher School which attracted a brilliant collection of civil servants, intellectuals and academics. It was Britain's most successful – but unsung – intelligence agency during the Second World War.

## Security services and the rule of law

According to A V Dicey, author of the constitutional bible, *An Introduction to the Study of the Law of the Constitution*, the two fundamental rules of the unwritten British Constitution are the sovereignty of Parliament and the rule of law. Dicey said:

> It means in the first place, the absolute supremacy or predominance of ordinary law as opposed to the influence of arbitrary power, and excludes the existence of arbitrariness, of prerogative, or even of wide discretionary authority on the part of government ... The rule of law in this sense excludes the idea of any exemption of officials or others from the duty of obedience to the law which governs other citizens.[7]

Lord Denning, former Master of the Rolls, appeared to be writing in this tradition when he stated in his 1963 report on the Profumo Affair that:

> The Security Service (MI5) in this country is not established by Statute nor is it recognised by Common Law. Even the Official Secrets Acts do not acknowledge its existence. *The members of the Security Service are, in the eye of the law, ordinary citizens with no powers greater than anyone else. They have no special powers of arrest such as the police have ... They cannot enter premises without the consent of the householder, even though they may suspect a spy is there* (our emphasis).[8]

But if this was supposed to be the position in law, it certainly has not been the reality. If it were so, there would have been no need for the Government to introduce its Security Service Act in 1989.

In what must now be the best-known passage in *Spycatcher*, Peter Wright described how 'for five years we bugged and burgled our way across London at the State's bequest, while pompous bowler-hatted civil servants in Whitehall pretended to look the other way.'[9] He described how John Cuckney – later to become Sir John, chairman of the Westland helicopter company – was responsible for MI5's training programme when Wright joined the service in

1955. Wright was told: 'The Security Service cannot have the normal status of a Whitehall department because its work very often involves transgressing propriety or the law.'[10]

The absence of any legal sanction of MI5 operations caused problems for Lord Donaldson, the Master of the Rolls, during the *Spycatcher* litigation. 'It is silly for us to sit here and say that the Security Service is obliged to follow the letter of the law, it isn't real,' he said in the Court of Appeal.[11]

To try to get round the difficulty, he went on: 'The missing link is possibly this. Of course, there has to be some control; probably the best yet devised is to say the Security Service is bound by a strict rule of the law, but to always bear in mind a prerogative power not to pursue criminal proceedings and a statutory power in the Director of Public Prosecutions to stop criminal prosecutions.'[12] That procedure, Donaldson said, could be perfectly properly used in appropriate cases. It was essential in the 'public interest' for MI5 officers to break the law in some ways and for such breaches not to be prosecuted. He set a limit, observing that 'murder is an entirely different matter'. But he distinguished between matters the law should not sanction and matters the media should not report. Outlining a hypothetical allegation that the Security Service was planning to assassinate the head of a friendly country, he concluded: 'There must be a public interest in that not being published, whether it is true or false.'[13]

Lord Donaldson's attempt to distinguish between what should and what should not be permitted was reflected in his ruling in February 1988 that the British media should be allowed to report the contents of *Spycatcher* (mainly on the grounds that the book had already been published and distributed throughout the rest of the world). 'It would be a sad day for democracy and the rule of law', he said, 'if the Service were ever to be considered above or exempt from the law of the land. And it is not.' But, he added: 'It is absurd to contend that *any* [his emphasis] breach of the law, whatever its character, will constitute such "wrongdoing" as to deprive the Service of the secrecy without which it cannot possibly operate.'

The time may have come, Lord Donaldson continued, when Parliament should 'regularise' the status of MI5.[14] The Government grasped the message. The day after the Queen's Speech opening the new session of Parliament in November 1988, it published its Security Service Bill which, with one tidy step, legalised MI5 bugging and burglary. It placed the Security Service 'within the law', legalising what was previously unlawful, making a nonsense of Denning's claim that MI5 officers were 'ordinary citizens'.

In the case of MI6, which does not officially exist, and GCHQ, there is still no charter governing their activities. The guidelines setting out the functions of the Police Special Branch, issued by the Home Office, were published only in 1984.

## The role of the executive

According to the formal constitutional position, ministers are responsible to Parliament for all the activities of all government officials, including members of the security and intelligence services. In practice, ministers cannot possibly know what their officials – and least of all, perhaps, those in the security services – are up to. These agencies, set up away from the chains of command of conventional government departments, cling to the tradition that they only tell ministers what, in their judgment, ministers 'need to know'.

The 1989 Security Service Act states that entering premises or burglary is illegal unless authorised by a warrant issued by the Secretary of State – a senior minister.[15] That is the official, formal, procedure and similar provisions are included for telephone-tapping in the 1985 Interception of Communications Act which in theory covers all agencies: MI6, GCHQ, and the SB as well as MI5.[16]

But under these existing procedures there is no sure way of knowing whether or not operations are conducted illegally – without warrants and without the minister's knowledge. There is also no sure way of knowing whether ministers themselves have kept to the statutory guidelines.

Even the prime minister's responsibility to appoint the head of MI5 can, in practice, be distorted. An illuminating example of how MI5 can bully a prime minister, when it comes to its top appointment, is recounted by Peter Wright in *Spycatcher*. Martin Furnival-Jones was due to retire as MI5 Director-General in 1972. Sir Philip Allen, the Permanent Secretary at the Home Office (now Lord Allen of Abbeydale, a member of the Security Commission) wanted an outsider to replace him. Sir Philip had become alarmed about MI5's cavalier use of immunities and the poor calibre of MI5 management. He suggested that Sir James Waddell, a deputy secretary at the Home Office and apparently a stickler for propriety – over the issuing of warrants, for example – should replace Sir Martin. Edward Heath, the Prime Minister, agreed.

MI5 was horrified by the prospect. Wright wrote: 'There were many secrets which MI5 had kept from their political and civil service masters, and the last thing anyone in MI5 wanted at that stage was the explosive story of the mole hunts to receive an airing around Whitehall.' MI5 officers enlisted the support of Lord Rothschild, head of Heath's think-tank, who had maintained a keen interest in MI5 ever since he had worked in intelligence in the war. MI5 got its way. Heath agreed to appoint its candidate – Sir Michael Hanley – during a weekend at Chequers where Rothschild successfully bent the Prime Minister's ear.[17]

## The role of the Attorney-General and Director of Public Prosecutions

Two lawyers who act for the executive are the Attorney-General and the Director of Public Prosecutions (DPP) – in Scotland their functions are performed by the Lord Advocate and the Procurator-Fiscal respectively. It is they who share responsibility for taking prosecutions relating to activities by the security services and to breaches of the Official Secrets Act.

According to the official Code for Crown Prosecutors, in cases where the final decision on a prosecution *formally* rests with the DPP, he or she must consider 'whether the public interest requires a prosecution'.[18] These guidelines were set by Lord Shawcross, who, when Attorney-General in 1951, told the Commons:

> It has never been the rule in this country – and I hope it never will be – that suspected criminal offences must automatically be the subject of prosecution. Indeed, the very first Regulations under which the Director of Public Prosecutions worked provided that he should prosecute 'wherever it appears that the offence or the circumstances of its commission is or are of such a character that a prosecution in respect thereof is required in the public interest'. That is still the dominant consideration. Regard must be had to the effect which the prosecution, successful or unsuccessful as the case may be, would have upon public morale and order, and with any other considerations affecting public policy.[19]

These criteria are imprecise, open to political as well as subjective interpretation. The attorney-general is at one and the same time a member of the government and an independent law officer. Before taking a decision, he or she is free – indeed, some say s/he is under a duty – to consult fellow members of the government. The post enjoys a wide measure of discretion. It is the attorney-general who advises the DPP not to proceed with a prosecution when s/he considers it would not be in 'the public interest' to do so. In practice, the attorney's influence can determine the final decision.

Early in 1988, in one of the most controversial decisions ever taken by an attorney-general, Sir Patrick Mayhew advised the Northern Ireland DPP not to prosecute senior officers of the Royal Ulster Constabulary despite evidence of attempts to pervert the course of justice during the Stalker inquiry into an alleged shoot-to-kill policy. His advice was accepted. Sir Patrick explained to the Commons that the DPP in Northern Ireland had decided not to prosecute RUC officers for reasons of 'public interest' and 'national security'.[20]

## The role of the judiciary

Despite their repeated references to the rights of the individual and the danger of accepting claims by the Executive at face value, senior judges have rarely challenged the government when it has raised the 'national security' flag. In his defence of the Labour Government's decision in 1977 to deport the American journalist, Mark Hosenball, despite the fact that no hard evidence had been provided against him, Lord Denning remarked: 'This is no ordinary case. It is a case in which national security is involved, and our history shows that when the state is endangered, our cherished freedoms may have to take second place.'[21]

In an unanimous Law Lords' ruling upholding the Government's decision to ban union membership at GCHQ in 1984, Lord Fraser, the senior Law Lord, stated:

> The decision on whether the requirements of national security outweigh the duty of fairness in any particular case is for the government and not for the courts. The government alone has access to the necessary information, and in any event the judicial process is unsuitable for reaching decisions on national security.[22]

The Law Lords added: 'Those who are responsible for the nation's security must be the sole judges of what the national security requires. It would be obviously undesirable that such matters should be made the subject of evidence in a court of law or otherwise discussed in public.'[23]

## The role of Parliament

Government – the executive – has been steadily eating away at Parliament's powers; sometimes it seems that Parliament's fights with the monarchy over the years were all for nothing. In many ways, Parliament had more effective control over government expenditure in centuries past than it does now. Two hundred years ago the monarch – the government – had to go to Parliament for funds to fight a war. Legislation controlled the amount of money the government could spend on the security and intelligence services.

Ten years ago, Robin Cook – then a Labour backbencher, now shadow social services secretary – discovered during research into MI5 accountability that the Civil List and Secret Service Act of 1782 prevented the government from spending more than £10,000 a year on secret services. The Act was repealed in 1977, after nearly two centuries of illegal overspending.[24]

Today, Parliament has no idea how much is spent on the security services. In December 1988, in answer to a question from a backbench MP, Norman Lamont, Financial Secretary to the Treasury, gave the one figure which is published in the annual Public Expenditure White Papers. The figure for the 'secret service vote', he said, would total £113.2 millions in 1988/89 – an increase of over 50 percent in four years. But this is only a small proportion of what is actually spent. Asked under what other headings expenditure on the intelligence services was accounted for, Lamont replied: 'In the interests of national security, successive governments have declined to publish the information requested.'[25]

The degree to which expenditure of the security and intelligence services is scrutinised is limited to the Comptroller and Auditor General – Parliament's financial watchdog – being sent a note from the Cabinet Secretary with an assurance that the money was properly spent. The all-party Commons Public Accounts Committee appears to accept this approach.

This secret expenditure is hidden in the budgets for the Contingencies Fund (which pays for unspecified and unforeseen expenditure), the Home Office, the Foreign Office and – in particular – the Ministry of Defence (MoD).[26] Most of GCHQ's expenditure is disguised in the MoD budget – the £500 million allocated for the planned Zircon spy satellite, for example, would have come out of the defence budget.

## *The Zircon project*

The 'Zircon incident' provides an illustration of Parliament's collusion in the executive's refusal to give MPs information on security matters. The Zircon project was first disclosed by the journalist, Duncan Campbell, who was the presenter of a programme for BBC2's 'Secret Society' series due to have been broadcast in 1987. Embarrassed by the disclosure, the Government obtained an injunction preventing the programme from being transmitted. The Special Branch raided the Glasgow offices of the BBC where the film was being edited, as well as Campbell's London home. The House of Commons Speaker (Bernard Weatherill) prevented MPs from seeing the film after MoD officials succeeded in stopping the Commons Defence Committee from watching it. Meanwhile, the Foreign Office persuaded the Labour Party leader, Neil Kinnock, and other Labour leaders that the film would indeed endanger 'national security' if it was shown.

Remarkably, Kinnock accepted the Government's argument without seeing the film for himself. Sir Peter Marychurch, the director of GCHQ, stated in an affidavit for the High Court that the film would harm Britain's future intelligence co-operation with the US. Yet a year later, the Government withdrew all its objections and the film was shown, uncut, in September 1988. Significantly, especially in light of the ruling of the Speaker, who is supposed to stand up for MPs' rights, Campbell's disclosure showed that the MoD had broken an agreement whereby the Commons Public Accounts Committee was to be informed in advance of all new major projects.[27]

## *No comment!*

In October 1988, Prime Minister Margaret Thatcher was reminded in the Commons that many MPs, including Conservative backbenchers, had repeatedly called for a committee of privy councillors to oversee the activities of the security and intelligence agencies. She replied: 'It has been the long standing convention, under Governments of both parties, that the security services are responsible to the appropriate Secretary of State and through them to the Prime Minister. I believe that the establishment of a Select Committee would not represent an improvement in these arrangements.'[28] Time and again ministers have met questions from MPs with the answer: 'It has been the general practice of successive governments not to comment on security policy.'[29] The Government has made it clear that the passing of the Security Service Act will not alter this almost uniquely British convention.

Both the Speaker and the Commons Table Office – which vets questions from MPs – have blocked queries about security and intelligence matters, even when these have already appeared in published books. For example, the Labour MP, Dale Campbell-Savours, put down a series of questions in 1987 relating to information disclosed in a book on GCHQ by Nigel West, pseudonym of the Tory MP for Torbay, Rupert Allason. Campbell-Savours was told by the principal clerk at the Commons Table Office, Donald Limon, that the Speaker agreed with his opinion that the questions 'do not comply with the rule about matters of their nature secret'.[30] He referred to Erskine May – the bible of parliamentary practice. This states that 'among the subjects on which successive administrations have refused to answer questions upon grounds of public policy are ... security matters including the operation of the security services ... Questions on these matters are not in order.'[31] The rules and conventions in Erskine May are set not by MPs, but by a committee of Commons' clerks – unelected officials.

In his *Governance of Britain*, published in 1977, the former Labour leader, Harold Wilson, wrote in what must be one of the shortest chapters ever written, headed 'The Prime Minister and National Security':

> The prime minister is occasionally questioned on matters arising out of his responsibility. His answers may be regarded as uniformly uninformative. There is no further information that can usefully or properly be added before bringing this Chapter to an end.[32]

He prefaced the chapter with a quote from Harold Macmillan, one of his predecessors. 'It is dangerous and bad', Macmillan had said, 'for our general national interest to discuss these matters'.[33] These words were repeated by Thatcher ten years later when she fought off pressure for an inquiry into the allegations that a group in MI5 had attempted to destabilise Wilson's government in the mid-1970s (see Chapter Six).

It is no exaggeration to say, in conclusion, that Parliament has no role at all in setting the expenditure, or monitoring the activities, of the security and intelligence services.

# CHAPTER TWO

# Official Secrets

Intelligence agencies have played a crucial role in shaping events; indeed, sometimes they have been their hidden cause. If Whitehall continues to have its way, we shall never know. The cloak of secrecy it wants to wrap around Britain's security and intelligence agencies even extends to the writing of history.

## Secrecy and official history

For more than ten years Mrs Thatcher sat on two official histories commissioned by the government before she came to power.[1] Elsewhere the situation is very different. Between 1977 and 1983, 170 former American intelligence officers submitted 430 articles and books to the Central Intelligence Agency's (CIA) Publication Review Board. Not a single work was prohibited although in some cases deletions were requested – on occasion at the insistence of Whitehall. For example, references to Britain's role in the toppling of the nationalist Iranian leader, Mossadeq, in 1953, were excised from *Countercoup* by the former CIA officer, Kermit Roosevelt. Cuts were also ordered in *The CIA and The Cult of Intelligence* by Victor Marchetti and John Marks, two former CIA agents, as a result of British sensitivities.[2]

There has also been no shortage of books on MI5, MI6 or about the wartime activities of the Government Code & Cypher School, the forerunner of GCHQ. A few were written without permission by participants frustrated by Whitehall's refusal to publish their successes. Some were discreetly vetted after the authors made informal approaches to their Whitehall contacts. Authors as well as newspaper editors are advised to consult the secretary of the D Notice committee, which runs a system of voluntary self-censorship, if they intend to write about security, intelligence, or defence issues.[3]

Some books have been written by authors on the basis of unauthorised interviews with former members of the security services. They include books by Niger West (the alias of Tory MP, Rupert Allason) and by Chapman Pincher, devoted to allegations of Soviet penetration of MI5 in the 1950s and 1960s.[4] Evidence in the *Spycatcher* trial that Whitehall knew in advance about these books but did nothing to stop them even though they contained damageing allegations (including the claim that Sir Roger Hollis, a former head of MI5, was a Soviet agent) was a major factor in the Government's defeat in the Australian courts. The Government's embarrassment also prompted it to impose (in the new Official Secrets Act) an absolute, life-long duty of silence on all former members of the security and intelligence services.

## *Cavendish's memoirs*

No sooner had the Government lost its case over *Spycatcher* than it was faced with another embarrassment. In 1987, Anthony Cavendish, an MI5 and MI6 officer in the 1940s and early 1950s, privately printed his memoirs, *Inside Intelligence*, and sent copies to some 350 friends as a Christmas present.[5] This short book described some operations going back to the 1950s. It consisted mainly of personal anecdotes and included a defence of his former friend, the ex-Chief of MI6, Sir Maurice Oldfield. Oldfield, victim of an MI5 smear campaign, had been described by the author and journalist, Chapman Pincher, as a homosexual who had indulged in rough trade.[6]

Extracts of *Inside Intelligence* appeared in newspapers. The Government immediately obtained a court injunction preventing further publication. However, after a High Court hearing, government lawyers agreed that the press could publish two-thirds of the book. This exercise undermined at a stroke the Government's argument that the duty of confidentiality binding former members of the security services was absolute and that the contents of any publication by them was irrelevant. The Government's attempt to stop Cavendish's book finally collapsed when the Law Lords ruled in 1989 that the media could publish the entire contents. They did so mainly because the Government admitted that publication would not harm national security. Despite this, government lawyers continued to maintain that Cavendish was still personally subject to an absolute duty of silence even though the media was absolutely free to publish what he had to say.

The then Home Secretary, Douglas Hurd, told the Conservative MP, Julian Amery, that in future, authority for any former officer to speak would be only given in 'rare and exceptional circumstances'.[7] The Official Secrets Act is designed to prevent any further embarrassing disclosures. It is already frightening publishers. It raises the question whether, had it been in force at the time, Andrew Boyle would have been able to expose Anthony Blunt as a Soviet agent in his book, *The Climate of Treason*, published in 1979.[8] Significantly, the only Tory peers who opposed the Act as it passed through the Lords in 1989 were historians – Lord Bethell, Lord (Hugh) Thomas, and Lord Dacre (Hugh Trevor-Roper).

## *The Welchman affair*

One telling episode illustrates the attitude of the intelligence bureaucracy under Margaret Thatcher. Shortly before he died of cancer in 1985 Gordon Welchman, a leading wartime cryptanalyst in charge of the Government Code and Cypher School's celebrated Hut 6 at Bletchley, wrote an article for a specialist journal, *Intelligence and National Security*.[9] Sir Peter Marychurch, the director of

GCHQ, was not amused. The article, he claimed, caused 'direct damage to security'. He went on: 'Each time a person like yourself of obviously deep knowledge and high repute, publishes inside information about the inner secrets of our work, there is more temptation and more excuse for others to follow suit.'[10]

His outburst provoked a curt response from Welchman's successor at Hut 6, Sir Stuart Milner-Barry. Sir Stuart described Marychurch's complaint as 'a prime example of the lengths to which GCHQ's paranoia about the preservation of ancient secrets will carry them.' To talk of 'direct damage to security', Sir Stuart commented, was 'surely absurd'. He added: 'To suppose that the battles which we had to wage before the birth of the first electronic computer (which must seem to present-day cryptanalysts rather like fighting with bows and arrows) could be relevant to security now is just not credible.'[11]

## *Cumming's log book*

Some facts which the security and intelligence bureaucracy do not want disclosed seem to be a product of fiction. The first chief, or 'C', of the Secret Intelligence Service (MI6), Sir Mansfield Cumming, wore a gold-rimmed monocle, wrote only in green ink and after losing part of his leg in an accident, moved around his office on a child's scooter. For him, it was a game played by adults. Trying to persuade the author Compton Mackenzie to stay on in MI6, he told him: 'Here, take this swordstick. I always took it with me on spying expeditions before the war. That's when this business was really amusing. After the war is over we'll do some amusing secret service work together. It's capital sport.'[12]

To this day, internal Whitehall correspondence to the Chief of the Secret Intelligence Service is addressed to 'C' – in green ink.

On January 25, 1989 – more than 65 years after Cumming's retirement – Roy Hattersley, the Shadow Home Secretary, referred in the House of Commons to a log book kept by the first head of MI6. Recently, he said, Cumming's family asked to see it just for sentimental reasons. He added: 'They were told that they could not see any of it or obtain the information they sought – the name of the theatrical costumier from whom Cumming bought his disguises. How would it be detrimental to the state if that information were given a wider audience?'[13] To John Patten, Minister of State at the Home Office, the matter was deadly serious. He replied: 'I will not comment on operational decisions taken by the service in the past. That is a tradition followed by governments of all political colours in respect of major and minor operational decisions. I hope that it will continue.'[14]

There is one reason why we shall *never* know about some past events. Documents are weeded and destroyed by officials accountable to no one. Among official papers recently shredded are those relating to Foreign Office advice to the Government before the Argentine invasion of the Falklands in 1982; British relations with the South African security and intelligence services; and the 1986 Westland affair – the controversy, which shook the Government, over who leaked part of a letter from the Solicitor-General.[15]

## Official leaks

The hypocrisy which has surrounded Whitehall's attitude towards official secrecy is particularly poignant in the field of security and intelligence. Contrast Marychurch's censorious attitude towards Welchman with the spectacular leak which helped to bring down Ramsay MacDonald's Labour Government 50 years earlier. On September 15, 1924, a letter purported to have been sent by Grigori Zinoviev, president of the Comintern, to the Communist Party of Great Britain, instructed their sympathisers in the Labour Party to 'strain every nerve' to ensure the ratification of the Anglo-Soviet Treaty (covering mainly commercial issues) and to encourage 'agitation-propaganda' in the armed forces. The letter was leaked to the *Daily Mail* and was published in that newspaper just four days before the general election on October 29.

There is little doubt that the letter, whether forged or genuine, was designed to help bring down the Labour Government. The chief conspirators in the plot were the Conservative Central Office – which paid for the letter – and a handful of retired intelligence officers. They included Sir Reginald 'Blinker' Hall, director of naval intelligence during the first world war, one of the founders of MI6 and of the private vetting agency the Economic League.[16] The plotters also included Lt. Colonel Freddie Browning, the wartime Deputy Chief of MI6 and a former principal agent at Conservative Central Office. According to the historian, Christopher Andrew, it was likely that they were given a copy of the letter by a sympathiser within the intelligence community, possibly Joseph Ball, an MI5 officer who later became the Conservative Party's Director of Publicity.[17]

A few years later, the Conservative Prime Minister, Stanley Baldwin, could not resist the temptation to disclose how the Government was successfully intercepting Soviet telegrams. He spilled the beans in 1927 when the Government needed evidence of Soviet espionage and political interference in Britain to justify breaking off diplomatic relations with Moscow. With this indiscretion, inspired by domestic politics, the Soviet Union was thus warned by the British Government to protect its secret communications more carefully. Yet fifty years later, in the famous ABC case (see Chapter Four), two journalists and a former soldier were charged with breaking the Official Secrets Act for describing how the Government was continuing to intercept foreign communications through GCHQ.[18]

A more recent episode exposing the double standards which surround official secrecy concerned the invitation to a former MI5 officer, Charles Elwell, to address the Conservative Party's backbench Home Affairs Committee in December 1987. The meeting was hurriedly cancelled after it was leaked to the press. It was just at the time the Government was claiming in the courts that former members of the security and intelligence services were bound by an absolute life-long duty of silence – a claim soon to be enshrined in the new Official Secrets Act. The Government had just obtained an injunction preventing BBC Radio 4 from transmitting 'My Country Right or Wrong', a series on the accountability of Western intelligence services. One of those the Government objected to speaking on the radio was John Day, a former senior MI5 officer who had been a regular adviser to MPs, including members of the Commons Defence Committee.

Charles Elwell was head of MI5's F1 section in the late 1970s and early 1980s, investigating 'Communist subversion'. In that capacity he designated the National Council for Civil Liberties, among other groups, a legitimate security service target.[19] He also set up a special MI5 unit to monitor the media for alleged subversion and left-wing bias. In 1983, Elwell wrote a pamphlet – published by the Social Affairs Unit and financed by the Institute of Economic Affairs – in which he listed and commented on a number of fringe, left-wing newspapers and magazines.[20]

Later Elwell was paid by David Hart, a friend and former adviser of Thatcher, to edit a clandestine tract called *British Briefing* (BB). The tract consists of pejorative comments about Labour and trade union personalities as well as pressure groups – including Shelter, which he described as having 'Communist affiliations' – and various charities, writers and playwrights. Among those BB has accused of helping the Communist cause are Bryan Gould, the shadow environment secretary, and Labour MPs Maria Fyfe (Glasgow, Maryhill), Harry Barnes (Derbyshire, North-East), and Chris Mullin (Sunderland South).

A discreet note at the back of *British Briefing* tells its recipients – selected MPs, industrialists and journalists – that while they may 'make free use of the information therein, they are asked to refrain from mentioning it, or its existence, and from direct quotation.'[21] Earlier in his career, Elwell had also run MI5's K2 branch dealing with Soviet satellite countries. He was closely involved in allegations made by defectors, notably the Czech, Josef Frolik, that some of Harold Wilson's associates – including John Stonehouse, then Postmaster-General – were Soviet agents.[22]

## Cover-ups

Official leaks notwithstanding, it has frequently been governments themselves which have been kept in the dark by the security services. One of the essential ingredients of Whitehall culture is the 'need to know' principle. Officials defend it on the grounds that the more you tell other officials – and ministers – the greater the likelihood of sensitive information being leaked. Another interpretation is that the reasons why officials promote this approach stems from bureaucratic traditions and power. The more people are informed, the greater the likelihood of activities being challenged and questioned.

Ministers, according to the Maxwell-Fyfe Directive, MI5's charter between 1952 and 1989 (see Chapter Three), should be given detailed information 'only as may be necessary for the determination of any issue on which guidance is sought'.[23] What information is given to the home secretary, or even the prime minister, is entirely at the discretion of the head of MI5. (The same, we can assume, applies to MI6 and GCHQ as well as the police.) Nothing in the Security Service Act changes this.

The former Labour Home Secretary, Merlyn Rees, has described how he was kept in the dark about the vetting of BBC staff as well as what MI5 was up to in Northern Ireland in the 1970s.[24] For his predecessor, Roy Jenkins, there was a different problem. Those who worked with him say he did not like to get involved in what he considered 'grubby' matters – MI5's activities. It is said that the former Prime Minister, Harold Macmillan, did not even know the names of the heads of MI5 or MI6 during the Profumo affair. Douglas Hurd suggested when he was Home Secretary that he was far from happy about the way MI5 had withheld information from ministers (and privately intimated his support for a system of independent accountability of MI5 during the debates in 1986 provoked by the *Spycatcher* affair). Lord Callaghan, who took a keen interest in security affairs when he was Prime Minister, acknowledged in 1987 that he did not feel as confident as he did in office that MI5 was under proper control. He said he did not enquire as much as he should have done about what it was up to.

Lord Callaghan has said he is in favour of a system of independent scrutiny of MI5. When asked by the Commons in 1986 about allegations that a group of MI5 officers had plotted against the Wilson administration and that MI5 was out of control, he replied:

> I think that depends on whether the prime minister exercises such control. I do not know what 'out of control' means, honestly I really do not. If it means do they take initiatives of their own kind without clearing everything with a minister, if it means that, the answer is, yes, of course they take such initiatives ... They sometimes put to a minister

actions which they think he will regard as repugnant but nevertheless they hope he will agree and the answer will be yes. Then it depends on the minister, whether he is sufficiently alert to say no to those particular questions.[25]

## *From Burgess to Blunt*

Sometimes ministers have been told about security and intelligence scandals or embarrassments but then kept them from Parliament. Sometimes ministers themselves have been kept in the dark. Often, when disclosures are made, they emerge late, enabling the government of the day to pass them off as history.

- Guy Burgess and Donald Maclean, the two Foreign Office spies, fled Britain in May 1951. It was not until 1955 – when they gave a press conference in Moscow – that the Government published a White Paper on their case.

- Selwyn Lloyd, Eden's Foreign Secretary, was unaware of MI6's plan to assassinate President Nasser in 1956.

- Macmillan tried to conceal the fact that George Blake, the MI6 agent who admitted spying for the Soviet Union in an Old Bailey trial held largely in secret in 1962, had ever worked for the Secret Intelligence Service. George Brown, Labour's deputy leader who had been told the truth under privy council rules, was so outraged by the cover-up that he leaked the story to the *Daily Express* journalist, Chapman Pincher.

- MI5 withheld from former Prime Minister Harold Macmillan its involvement with Stephen Ward before the Profumo affair became an embarrassing – and, for the Government, a damageing – scandal in 1963.

- The Government did not admit that Kim Philby had been a double agent until after he fled to the Soviet Union from Beirut in 1963, more than 12 years after he was suspected of being so by MI5 and had retired from MI6.

- Christopher Chataway, the then Minister of Posts and Telecommunications, was not told about a new telephone-tapping system introduced by GCHQ and MI5 in co-operation with the Post Office in the early 1970s.

- The then Prime Minister, Sir Alec Douglas-Home, was not told that Anthony Blunt had confessed to being a Soviet agent in return for immunity from prosecution in 1964, and there is some doubt as to whether the Queen was informed by her private secretary. Margaret Thatcher put it this way when she made her statement on Blunt to the Commons on November 21, 1979:

> The Home Secretary of the day, now Lord Brooke, who, at first, did not recall being told, has been reminded of these meetings and has, with characteristic integrity, accepted that his memory must have been at fault ... There was therefore no failure on the part of the Security Service to carry out its duty to inform the Home Secretary of these matters. It was for the Home Secretary to decide whether the Prime Minister should be informed. Neither Lord Brooke nor Lord Home can recall discussing the matter.[26]

Blunt kept on his job as Surveyor of the Queen's Pictures. Although the Queen's advisers were told of Blunt's past as a Soviet agent, it seems the Queen was kept in the dark.

Blunt's treachery came to light only through *The Climate of Treason* by Andrew Boyle, published in 1979.[27] But if MI5 and Whitehall had had their way, Thatcher would have kept quiet. Sir Robert Armstrong, her Cabinet Secretary, tried in vain to prevent her from disclosing the deal. MI5, he told the Prime Minister, was worried that if the Blunt deal was exposed, other moles offered immunity in return for a confession would not trust the Government to keep it quiet.

Shortly afterwards, the Labour MP Robin Cook – then a backbencher – introduced his own Bill to make MI5 accountable to Parliament. Introducing the Bill – which inevitably fell – Cook noted: 'The debate on Mr Blunt concentrated on the question whether the Security Service is properly accountable to ministers. That missed the point. It does not matter very much whether the security services are answerable to a minister when that minister is not answerable to the House.'[28]

Blunt's exposure – and the reaction to it – in 1979 forced the Government to withdraw its Protection of Official Information Bill, its first attempt to reform the 1911 Official Secrets Act. The Bill would have prevented authors and journalists from disclosing any information about the activities of the security and intelligence agencies. The Blunt deal would have remained a secret. Ten years later, Parliament appears to have brushed this episode aside – under the 1989 Official Secrets Act, the Blunt affair would have remained under wraps for, as we have seen, it too imposes a blanket ban on unauthorised disclosures about the security and intelligence services.

## *Scandals and spies*

The Blunt affair strengthened Margaret Thatcher's determination to take close personal supervision of security and intelligence matters. But two years later in 1981, she was faced with another embarrassing episode which was to show that MI5 and MI6 were still withholding information from both the Prime Minister and the Cabinet Secretary, Sir Robert (now Lord) Armstrong.

It emerged during the *Spycatcher* trial in Sydney in 1986 that both MI5 and Sir Arthur Franks – the former head of MI6 and contact of Chapman Pincher – knew about the forthcoming Pincher book *Their Trade is Treachery* three months before it was published.[29] But Armstrong told the court that he and Mrs Thatcher were only told about the book just three weeks before it was published. As we have seen, MI5's delay in informing the Government, and the Government's failure to do anything to stop the book, were some of the main reasons why the Australian courts dismissed the Government's attempt to ban *Spycatcher*. The argument was that since the Government had done nothing to stop Pincher's book, there was no reason why *Spycatcher* – which contained much of the same information – should be banned. In a telling statement to the New South Wales Supreme Court, Armstrong conceded that he could think of nothing more damageing to MI5 than the allegation – contained in Pincher's book – that Sir Roger Hollis, one of its former chiefs, had been a Soviet spy.

It later emerged that Pincher had arranged for an anonymous middle-man to send a copy of the manuscript of *Their Trade is Treachery* to MI5 and that he was prepared to warn the publishers, Sidgwick & Jackson, if MI5 objected. No objection was forthcoming. Armstrong told the High Court in London in December 1987 that he had not been aware of this arrangement at the time of the Sydney trial – that is to say, more than five years after the arrangement was made. Armstrong, Thatcher's most senior adviser on the security services, showed in the trial that he himself was ignorant about the basis on which the decision not to stop the Pincher book had been taken. He had to apologise to the court after the then Attorney-General, Sir Michael Havers, insisted that Armstrong's claim that he (Havers) had been responsible for the decision was false.

It was also revealed during the Sydney trial that MI5 was aware that Granada Television was planning an interview with Wright in May 1984 – two months before it was broadcast – but did not tell the Government and did nothing to stop the programme.

Thatcher made a statement on Hollis to the Commons on March 26, 1981. It was far from complete and, in some ways, misleading. She said that all of the leads suggesting Hollis might have been an agent could have been explained 'by reference to Philby or Blunt'.[30] Wright later described the statement as 'a masterly piece of Whitehall deception'.[31] In particular, he argued that the leads relating to possible continuing Soviet penetration had emerged long after Philby and Blunt had had access to secrets. Other former MI5 officers agree with Wright about this.

Armstrong himself confirmed that there had been evidence of post-war Soviet penetration of MI5 which could not have been attributed to Philby or Blunt. He conceded: 'The Prime Minister's statement did not refer explicitly to matters considered in the course of the investigation which suggested there was continued high-level penetration of British counter-intelligence after the last years of the war'.[32] He explained away the gaps in Thatcher's statement by saying 'there are limits to the length of an oral statement that could be made. It was comprehensive in terms of what can be expected in an oral statement to Parliament.'[33] Ironically, the US Congress was informed about the allegations against Hollis, and the reasons for them, long before the House of Commons.

## Bungling and bureaucracy

The issue of the penetration of the security services by double agents cannot be looked at in isolation from the overall way they are run. The absence of accountability covers up inefficiency, poor management and corruption in the security and intelligence services – as it does in any bureaucracy. And without outside scrutiny, there is no incentive to learn from past mistakes. There is no self-examination.

A former GCHQ radio operator, Jock Kane, campaigned for many years against what he described as 'a disgusting network of corruption, inefficiency and security betrayal' in the intelligence-gathering centre, and particularly its base at Little Sai Wan in Hong Kong. His allegations led to the conviction of a senior Ministry of Defence official in the colony. But a security investigation conducted by Sir James Waddell (the former senior Home Office official excluded by the MI5 establishment in the early 70s as a future head of the Security Service) was pigeon-holed by top GCHQ management at Cheltenham. After resigning under pressure in 1978, Kane wrote a book which he called *GCHQ – A Negative Asset*. In 1984 Special Branch officers seized the manuscript on behalf of government lawyers who succeeded in obtaining a court injunction banning the book. It was the first time the Government used the civil law of confidence rather than the Official Secrets Act to suppress information (it was later to use the same legal device against Peter Wright's *Spycatcher*). The Attorney-General's office described Kane's book as 'an account given by him of information that by its nature is confidential and represents a breach of his duty of confidence to the Crown'.[34]

Kane alleged that widespread negligence at GCHQ created conditions which enabled Geoffrey Prime, a Russian linguist who passed a series of positive vetting investigations, to smuggle thousands of pages of top secret material out of GCHQ during the 1970s. He alleged that Prime compromised a sensitive detection system – codenamed Sambo – used to locate Soviet ballistic missile submarines when they surfaced to communicate with their bases.

Prime was arrested in 1982 by the West Mercia police for child molesting. It was during a search of his house that the police found spying equipment. In November of that year, he was sentenced to 35 years in prison after a trial conducted largely in secret.

The most damning indictment of MI5's management came in a report by the Security Commission on Michael Bettaney in 1985. A year earlier, Bettaney, then 34, was sentenced to 23 years in prison for sending information to the Soviet embassy. He was the first MI5 officer to face trial under the old Official Secrets Act. Despite ample evidence of serious character defects, Bettaney kept his positive vetting clearance. Over a number of years he had advertised his own doubts and personal problems in drinking bouts during which he chided his colleagues with such comments as 'I'm sure the East Germans would look after me better.' He began to drink heavily at the beginning of 1976 during a period when both his parents died and after he had himself expressed doubts about his suitability for a posting described in the Commission's report as 'an operational role involving a high degree of stress'. The Security Commission did not disclose the posting in the part of its report which was published. The passage in the report was, in fact, a reference to Northern Ireland. During his posting there, Bettaney was injured in a car-bomb attack and, in another incident, hid in a house while in the next room his informant was having his knee-caps broken.

The Security Commission (described in the next chapter) said in its report on the affair:

> No doubt security considerations dictate that the [security] service should be to a large extent a self-contained and substantially autonomous organisation. But the very fact of the service's comparative isolation makes it all the more important that those responsible at the higher levels of management should maintain a self-critical attitude and be constantly alert to the need to keep the service's organisation, practices and procedures under review.[35]

Shortly after the report was published, MI5's Director-General, Sir John Jones – the first head of MI5 to have spent most of his career in F branch, responsible for 'domestic subversion' – took early retirement. He was replaced by Sir Antony Duff, Mrs Thatcher's trusted security and intelligence co-ordinator and former Foreign Office diplomat.

The Security Commission's report on the Bettaney affair raises the central questions of whether MI5 management could ever be sufficiently 'self-critical' and who should keep the organisation 'under review'. No outside body is doing it now. The Home Office says the Home Secretary can do it. This has been questioned even by former senior MI5 officers. In a memorandum to selected MPs and peers during the debates on the Security Service Bill in early 1989, John Day, a former senior MI5 officer, stated that to claim – as the Government did throughout the debates in both the Commons and the Lords – that MI5 could be properly accountable to ministers, was to fly in the face of the evidence and was wholly unrealistic. For a start, ministers did not have the time. 'Responsibility and accountability depend on accurate, timely information, and it is questionable to what extent this has been available to ministers in the past,' Day said.[36]

## The Official Secrets Act 1989

The new Official Secrets Act (OSA) will make it even more difficult for malpractice and mistakes to come to light whilst making it more likely that ministers themselves will be kept in the dark. With the extra bulwark provided by the Act, officials will be tempted to keep embarrassing events from ministers. The less the likelihood of embarrassing information being disclosed to MPs or the public, the less the likelihood of ministers being informed.

The jury's unanimous acquittal in 1985 of Clive Ponting – who was charged with sending information to the Labour MP, Tam Dalyell, about the circumstances surrounding the sinking of the Argentine cruiser, *Belgrano*, during the Falklands conflict – shocked the Government. It was the final nail in the coffin of the 'catch-all' Section 2 of the 1911 Official Secrets Act which said the disclosure of any official information without authority was a potential criminal offence (although, as we have seen, Section 1 remains in force). The discredited Act was one of the reasons why the Government took no action against the former MI5 officer, Cathy Massiter, who exposed MI5 operations in 1985. The Government was finally forced to seize the initiative when it blocked an attempt by the Tory backbencher, Richard Shepherd, to reform the Official Secrets Act in 1988. It would draw up one of its own, it told its supporters in the Commons. It was determined that the new Act would prevent any future Massiters or *Spycatcher* authors.

Under the OSA, any disclosure about any past or present activity of MI5 (or the other security and intelligence agencies), however noxious, damageing, or illegal, risks a criminal prosecution. The OSA imposes an absolute, life-long, duty of confidentiality on present and former members of the security and intelligence services (see Appendix I).

The notion of a blanket ban was first presented by Robert Armstrong. It was firmly rejected by the courts. 'I found myself unable to escape the reflection that the absolute protection of the security service that Sir Robert was contending for could not be achieved this side of the Iron Curtain,' Mr Justice Scott said in his December 1987 judgment dismissing the Government's attempt to ban Peter Wright's memoirs. He added: 'The ability of the press freely to report allegations of scandals in government is one of the bulwarks of our democratic society.'[37]

Unperturbed, the Government went ahead and included in criminal law what judges had rejected in civil law. The Act failed to include the principle of a 'public interest defence', allowing officials or editors to claim in court that they had made a disclosure to reveal crime, serious misconduct or abuse of authority. Such a principle – distancing the public or national interest from the interest of the government of the day – had been included in every previous Official Secrets Act, from 1889 onwards.

In a last attempt to get the Government's support for the principle of a public interest defence the Opposition, supported by a handful of Tory peers, proposed an amendment whereby officials would have to *prove* that their disclosures revealed 'serious misconduct involving crime, fraud or other gross impropriety'. They would have to go through all the internal complaints procedures before disclosing information to the outside world. The rejection of this prompted Lord Dacre – the Tory peer better known as the historian Hugh Trevor-Roper – to accuse the Government of dismissing the central argument in Britain's case against Nazi leaders at the Nuremburg war crimes trials:

> One goes to one's superiors in order to take counsel, and in the last resort one may go public under this amendment if one is satisfied that crime has been committed. Well, hang it all, what argument did we use at Nuremburg? We argued that criminality is not excused by superior orders. Therefore someone in a subordinate position who considers that real crime has been committed has a duty not to comply with it, not to obey those orders. Here in this amendment we are offering a mechanism whereby that predicament can be resolved.
>
> There is the argument that those who go into the secret services go in with their eyes open; they go in under special rules, etc. I do not want to make invidious comparisons, but simply looking at it as an abstract theory that is precisely the argument used by the SS. They said that they had a completely different set of rules. They went in with their eyes open. They did not obey the laws of the land. They were under different laws.[38]

## *Critique of the Act*

This absolute ban on disclosures about the security and intelligence services applies not only to present and former members of the services but also to other officials whom the government notifies must be bound by the same constraints because of the nature of their work. And the absolute ban on the disclosure of information about telephone-tapping, bugging or burglary by MI5 or GCHQ applies to the media as well as to all government officials.

This, coupled with the absence of a public interest defence – allowing an official, for example, to argue that he or she made a disclosure to reveal illegal acts – means that, uniquely in criminal law, a person can be convicted without any defence at all. The government will be able to instruct a jury to convict merely on its say-so that the accused was guilty of an absolute offence.

The Act also covers information relating to defence and international relations. In these cases there is no absolute ban. The government would have to show that a disclosure caused damage or was likely to. But the 'damage tests' – the criteria that could trigger off a criminal prosecution – are weaker even than those proposed in earlier attempts to reform the official secrets legislation. For a prosecution to be brought the government would only have to claim that a disclosure relating to defence or international relations could 'endanger the interests of the United Kingdom abroad' or 'seriously obstructs the promotion or protection of those interests' (or was likely to). In fact it would be enough for the government to claim that a disclosure of information relating to international relations was damageing, not because of its substance but because of the mere fact that it was 'confidential'. The key refrain in the Act is the reference to disclosures made 'without lawful authority'. It will be entirely up to the government's discretion how this will be interpreted.

# CHAPTER THREE

# How Targets are Defined

The characterisation of groups or activities as 'subversive' or as a threat to 'national security' lies at the heart of the operational judgments of the security and intelligence services. Moreover, these are words which, as we have seen, the government frequently relies on to justify its stance on security service matters. Yet they remain ill-defined, vague and highly ambiguous terms.

## 'Subversion'

There is no definition of 'subversion' in English law; it is not a crime. The term, as spelt out in the Special Branch (SB) guidelines and the Security Service Act, is wide open to subjective interpretation. The dangers were eloquently described by John Alderson, former Chief Constable of Devon and Cornwall, in evidence to the Commons Home Affairs Committee which conducted a rather half-hearted inquiry into the Special Branch in 1984. Although he was referring to the SB, his comments can apply equally to MI5. Alderson said:

> The terms of reference of the Special Branches leave much to their discretion. Some officers have a much wider understanding of the term 'subversive' than others. To some, all activists may be 'subversive' and both individuals and groups critical of the established order are marked out for surveillance and recording. Others, including myself, believe that although 'subversion' may not be capable of exact definition, if it is to be the subject of police operations, it should have an obvious criminal connection.[1]

He added when questioned by MPs:

> Policemen put constructions on situations which often may not suit other people's views. I think the difficulty is the interested citizen does not know what the State considers to be subversive. If we could stand up and say to the public in Devon and Cornwall, or anywhere else, 'this is what we consider to be subversive and if you start getting into this area of human activities you render yourself liable to surveillance' – but if you cannot tell the public that, it seems to me that people's liberties are likely to be at risk.[2]

But other senior policemen have given a different perspective. In 1981 Harold Salisbury, a former Yorkshire Chief Constable and then Commissioner of the

South Australian police, was asked by BBC 'Panorama' whom he would consider a 'subversive'. He replied:

> Obviously anyone who shows any affinity towards Communism – that's common sense. The IRA, the PLO and, I would say, anyone who's decrying marriage, family life – trying to break that up – pushing drugs, advocating the acceptance of certain drugs, homosexuality, indiscipline in schools, weak penalties for anti-social crimes, pushing that sort of thing. Oh, a whole gamut of things like that that could be pecking away at the foundations of our society and weakening it.[3]

The prevailing ethos of MI5 and the Special Branch reflects such illiberal values. Miranda Ingram has said of her former colleagues in MI5 that their overall tone was rightwing.[4] The former Conservative Prime Minister, Edward Heath, whilst praising the integrity of some of the MI5 officers he had come across, said that others were different. 'I met people in the Security Services', he told a surprised but entertained Commons, 'who talked the most ridiculous nonsense and whose philosophy was ridiculous nonsense. If some of them were on a tube and saw someone reading the *Daily Mirror* they would say: "Get him, that is dangerous. We must find out where he bought it."'[5]

Roy (now Lord) Jenkins, the former Labour Home Secretary, said during the controversy over the allegations contained in *Spycatcher:*

> I took the view before these recent events emerged that it was advisable that MI5 should be pulled out of its political surveillance role. I had been doubtful of the value of that role for some time. I am convinced now that an organisation of people who lived in the fevered world of espionage and counter-espionage is entirely unfitted to judge between what is subversion and what is legitimate dissent.

Nor, he continued,

> is the associated political intelligence role worthwhile, in my view. The object of this is presumably to help ministers with useful information. In my experience, however, the organisation wastes a great deal of ministers' time in dealing with its own peccadilloes, which detracts from any benefit which it provides.[6]

Other politicians have made it clear they did not share this view. William (now Viscount) Whitelaw stated when he was Home Secretary that the preservation of public order 'may require information to be kept on individuals who are active in a political movement, not because of the views they hold, but because the activities of the group could be such as to encourage public disorder.'[7]

Leon Brittan, Whitelaw's successor, who gave the go-ahead to MI5 to target the Campaign for Nuclear Disarmament (CND) in 1983, confessed in a letter two years later to the Labour MP, John Prescott:

> The definition [of subversion] is not limited to possible acts of a criminal nature. In an open society such as ours it is all too easy to use tactics which are not themselves unlawful for subversive ends. Those who are entrusted with safeguarding our democratic institutions from subversive attack must not be prevented from looking into the activities of those whose real aim is to harm democracy but who, *for tactical or other reasons choose to keep (either in the long or the short term) within the letter of the law in what they do* [our emphasis].[8]

This approach was echoed by his successor, Douglas Hurd, during the debates on the Security Service Bill. 'It is not sensible', he told the Commons on December 15, 1988, 'to define subversion only in terms of those who breach the criminal law. We must be able to know the plans and intentions of those who abuse the freedom that we provide under the law to infiltrate our institutions and structures.' The Security Service, he added, should take an interest 'only in people who have a deliberate purpose and intent to undermine parliamentary democracy and who also represent a real threat to the security of the nation'.[9]

Clear evidence that the Government wants a free hand both to collect information on 'subversives' and to prevent targeted individuals or groups from having access to the information held on them emerged in 1987 when member countries of the Council of Europe drew up a formal recommendation 'regulating the use of personal data in the public sector'. Britain was the only country which refused to accept the prohibition on collecting 'data on individuals solely on the basis that they have a particular racial origin, particular religious convictions, sexual behaviour or political opinions or belong to particular movements or organisations which are not proscribed by law.'[10]

The British Government also reserved its right not to comply with the principle that 'where data concerning an individual have been collected and stored without his knowledge, and unless the data are deleted, he should be informed, where practicable, that information is held about him as soon as the object of the police activities is no longer likely to be prejudiced.'[11]

As we shall show in more detail in Chapter Seven, Britain's allies have tried to meet the problem another way. Both the Australian and Canadian security services have abandoned the use of the term 'subversion', a decision which as far as the Canadian Security and Intelligence Service (CSIS) was concerned, meant doing away with a large operational branch. Alan Wrigley, former Director-General of the Australian Security Intelligence Organisation (ASIO), has frequently stated that the public did not expect its security services to be concerned with left-wing trade unions and other political activities. The definition of the word 'subversive', he has said, could be endless. Paule Gauthier, a lawyer and member of Canada's independent Intelligence Review Committee, told a meeting of the Anglo-American Ditchley Foundation – which organises conferences for members of 'the establishment' – at Ditchley Park, Oxfordshire in 1988: 'We discovered that there was no definition – certainly no definition acceptable to us – of the word "subversion".' She added: 'But that word is used throughout the English-speaking world to cover a multitude of sins.'[12]

By a process of some rigorous and careful thought, her committee came to the conclusion that, as she put it, 'all activities which we could envisage as being threats to the security of Canada were capable of being categorised ... precisely enough to eliminate any further need for a category under the rubric "subversion".' She added:

> It was only as we became more experienced, and as we examined files, voluminous files, in greater depth, that we began to realise that the word 'subversion', indeed the very concept of 'subversion', was used most of the time to cover a lack of rigorous thought and to camouflage its inevitable result, woolly language.[13]

The Ditchley conference was chaired by Lord Hunt, a former Cabinet Secretary, and participants included Sir Dick White, a former head of both MI5 and MI6, and Lord Bridge, a Law Lord and former chairman of the Security Commission. The official report of the meeting noted that concern had been expressed about '"subversion", a term which, it was generally agreed, was unsatisfactory because it was too wide and too vague'.[14]

The British Government has approached the problem from the opposite direction and has come to the opposite conclusion, the one that appears to suit it best. While other countries try to restrict and define the activities of their security services, Whitehall wants to allow MI5 to have an open-ended mandate. Any tighter definition in the Security Service Bill, any attempt to describe a 'comprehensive breakdown' of MI5's role, Hurd told the Commons, may prevent the agency from 'moving into new spheres' if necessary. Legislation, he went on, must say 'what the Security Service can do rather than what it cannot do'.[15] The Government even rejected an amendment drawn up by senior Conservative and Liberal Democrat MPs that would have excluded 'lawful advocacy, protest or dissent' from the definition of what should be regarded as a threat to 'national security'.[16]

## 'National security'

British governments have never paid much attention to the concept of 'national security' and how it should be defined or qualified. When questioned, ministers respond along the following lines: 'This term is generally understood to refer to the safeguarding of the state and the community against threats to their survival or well-being.' In January 1988, for example, Thatcher offered this form of words to the Labour MP, Ken Livingstone, to which she added: 'I am not aware that any previous administration has thought it appropriate to adopt a specific definition of the term.'[17] Yet the phrase is the first to be used to describe the functions of the security and intelligence services, as though it needs no further explanation. The Government also uses it to defend specific actions – for example the ban on union membership at GCHQ. Union membership there, Thatcher said, is incompatible with 'national security'.[18]

The Security Service Act states that 'the function of the Service shall be the protection of national security', adding, 'in particular' – but not exclusively – 'protection against threats from espionage, terrorism and sabotage, from the activities of agents of foreign powers' and 'from actions intended to overthrow or *undermine* parliamentary democracy by *political*, *industrial* or violent means' – now the established definition of subversion (our emphasis).[19]

'National security' is not defined in the Security Service Act. Nor is it defined in the Data Protection Act, where a 'national security exemption' allows government agencies and the police to refuse to disclose personal information which is held on computer. Nor, as Lord Justice Lloyd, the telephone-tapping commissioner, noted in his latest annual report published in March 1989, is it defined in the 1985 Interception of Communications Act.

'It is narrower,' Lloyd said, than the term 'public interest', but it was 'obviously wider than the three heads of counter-terrorism, counter-espionage and counter subversion.' The easiest example, he suggested, was defence. 'So if an interception is judged necessary for the defence of the realm against a potential external aggressor, then clearly it is necessary in the interests of national security.' But that was as far as Lloyd was prepared to go. It was neither wise nor possible, he said, to go further in attempting to define the term. 'Each case', he concluded, 'must be judged on its merits.' That is what the Home Secretary did and that was what he himself intended to do. In the end, it is all a matter of discretion.[20]

But in a White Paper on the interception of communications issued on February 7, 1985, the Home Office said:

> The Secretary of State may issue warrants on grounds of national security if he considers that the information to be acquired under the warrant is necessary in the interests of national security either because

> of terrorist, espionage or major subversive activity, *or in support of the Government's defence and foreign policies* (our emphasis).[21]

This suggests that any individual or group opposed to current government defence and foreign policies – its attitude to nuclear weapons, for instance, or towards the European Community – could be regarded as a legitimate target for surveillance or vetting by the security services.

## State security vetting

Historically Britain has avoided the overtly political purges of the McCarthyite era in the US. But pressure from Washington, especially after the arrest of the atom spy, Klaus Fuchs, in 1950, and the flight to the Soviet Union of the two Foreign Office officials, Burgess and Maclean in 1951, led Whitehall to introduce a positive vetting (PV) system in Britain. The principle of PV, covering civil servants and others working in what is regarded as sensitive areas of work, was introduced by Attlee in 1951. PV investigations, then as now, involve checking MI5 files as well as interviews with applicants' families and friends.

But MI5 not only helps to investigate the 66,000 or so civil servants and employees of the nuclear industry, British Telecom, defence companies and police forces who are aware that they are subject to positive vetting. It also plays a decisive role for those – estimated to involve at least 700,000 posts – whose appointments are dependent on whether they escape negative vetting. Unlike positive vetting, these checks are secret, made without the knowledge of the people concerned, to see whether MI5 has anything about them on their files. This is referred to in Whitehall as the 'nothing known against' procedure.[22]

The dangers for individual rights inherent in the vetting programme quickly became apparent. A committee of privy councillors, set up to look at security procedures in the public service, reported in 1956: 'It is right to continue the practice of tilting the balance in favour of offering greater protection to the security of the State rather than in the direction of safeguarding the rights of the individual.'[23]

One of the first victims of the formal PV system was Alan Turing, a brilliant mathematician who, more than any other single individual, enabled the Government Code & Cypher School to break the German Enigma code – an achievement which saved many lives during the second world war. A homosexual, Turing committed suicide in 1952 following pressure by the authorities after he resisted a blackmail attempt and reported it to the police.

## *The Radcliffe Report 1962*

The Portland spy ring affair[24] and the arrest of the double agent, George Blake,[25] led the Macmillan Government – anxious, like all its successors, to demonstrate that it was taking a constructive initiative after embarrassing scandals – to set up a new inquiry into security procedures under the Law Lord, Lord Radcliffe. It proposed stricter vetting and purge procedures in the Civil Service and the targeting of those who had, or were suspected of having had, Communist associations or sympathies. Relevant information, it noted, was most likely to be derived from intelligence records. The 'sources from which the main threat to security comes', his report said, 'are subversive organisations in this country, of which in current conditions the most formidable is the Communist Party of Great Britain, with its fringe of associated bodies and sympathisers.'[26]

The tone and intellectual contortions in the report are explicit. 'For the sake of brevity', it said, 'we have followed the common practice of using the phrase "communist" throughout to include fascists.' Yet it also acknowledged that 'it is not the policy of the [Communist] Party, according to our information, to give its members, open or secret, any encouragement to undertake espionage ... The Party is treated as one of a number of political parties seeking the votes of the electorate.'[27]

## *The Security Commission Report 1982*

Twenty years after the Radcliffe Report was published, the Security Commission – a body consisting of a senior judge, former civil servants and armed forces officers with no independent role – was asked by Thatcher to review security procedures. This was in the wake of the claim made by Chapman Pincher in his book *Their Trade is Treachery* that the former head of MI5, Sir Roger Hollis, was a Soviet agent.[28] The Commission did not investigate the validity of this claim, or the full facts that lay behind Thatcher's statement to the Commons in March 1981 which dismissed it. (As we have seen, former MI5 officers who were involved in the investigations say that the Prime Minister's statement was misleading.)

According to the edited version of the Security Commission's report presented by Thatcher to Parliament, the Commission found:

> The internal threat has altered considerably since Radcliffe. It has become more varied and viewed as a whole has grown more serious ... The threat offered by the Communist Party of Great Britain (CPGB), upon which Radcliffe concentrated, has probably diminished as a result of the fall in the number of its members and the disillusionment of many of them with Soviet policy since 1961 in invading Czechoslovakia and, more recently, Afghanistan. The fall in CPGB membership,

> however, has been accompanied by the proliferation of new subversive groups of the extreme Left and extreme Right (mainly the former) whose aim is to overthrow democratic parliamentary government in this country by violent or other unconstitutional means, not shrinking in the case of the most extreme groups from terrorism to achieve their aims. Membership of individual groups is small but, for the most part, active and conspiratorial. They might well seek to make public information injurious to the interests of this country, not at the behest or for the benefit of any foreign power, but simply to harm this country itself, whether by causing a rift between it and its allies or otherwise, and by these means to weaken its defences against the overthrow of democratic government by force.[29]

The report of the Security Commission, then chaired by Lord Diplock, reflected the growing interest of the security services in left-wing organisations, including trade unions and protest groups. This significant shift of emphasis began in the early 1970s and continued in the 1980s.

## *The 1985 guidelines on security vetting*

On the afternoon of April 3, 1985, just three hours before the parliamentary Easter recess, Thatcher announced new security vetting, or 'purge' procedures, in a written answer to the House of Commons. The timing and method of the sudden announcement meant that the Prime Minister could not be questioned by MPs about the new guidelines which had far-reaching implications. They would, she said, have 'immediate effect'.[30] The new procedures were to apply not only to the country's 600,000 civil servants but also the many thousands of staff employed by the nuclear industry, defence contractors, police forces, British Telecom and the Post Office.

The key feature of the guidelines is the new and broader definition of 'subversion' which goes well beyond that used by Lord Denning in his 1963 report on the Profumo affair. He described a 'subversive' as someone who 'would contemplate the overthrow of government by *unlawful* means' (our emphasis).

The 1985 guidelines state:

> It is the policy of Her Majesty's Government that no one should be employed in connection with work the nature of which is vital to the security of the state who:
>
> 1. Is, or has recently been, a member of a communist or fascist organisation, or of a subversive group, *acknowledged to be such*

*by the minister*, whose aims are to undermine or overthrow parliamentary democracy in the United Kingdom of Great Britain and Northern Ireland by *political, industrial or violent means.*

2. Is, or has recently been, *sympathetic to or associated with* members or sympathisers of such organisations or groups, in such a way as to raise reasonable doubts about his reliability.
3. Is susceptible to pressure from such organisations or groups (our emphases).[31]

The Government argued that these new guidelines merely reflected the concerns expressed by the Security Commission back in 1982. But the Commission had referred to the overthrow of democratic parliamentary government by violent or other unconstitutional means – criteria that while open to interpretation are nevertheless narrower than the 1985 guidelines. A more likely explanation for the initiative is that the Government was anxious to defend and give a kind of legitimacy to, the activities of MI5 – including the targeting of trade union leaders, the National Council for Civil Liberties (*Liberty*) and the Campaign for Nuclear Disarmament (CND) – that were exposed on television by the former Security Service officer, Cathy Massiter, just a month earlier.

The Government also argued that the definition of 'subversion' in paragraph one of the 1985 guidelines merely adopted the form of words used in a speech by Lord Harris of Greenwich, then a junior Home Office minister, in a Lords debate in 1975.[32] At the time, however, Lord Harris's phrase was regarded as no more than an off-the-cuff statement. This (1985) was the first occasion the guidelines had been used by a politician in the House of Commons and they had never been the subject of any debate. The guidelines in fact employ the broad definition of 'subversion' which had traditionally been used by MI5 and the Special Branch, unbeknown to either the public or Parliament. They were not even introduced as a result of stated government policy.

Groups and individuals unrelated to MI5's traditional target of Communists and foreign agents in Britain had been monitored for many years. Thatcher's statement in 1985, however, provided the first official acknowledgment that MI5's net was spreading even wider. Moreover, it indicated that ministers, and ministers alone, now judge what behaviour, attitudes or beliefs are to be regarded as 'subversive' as well as the kind of activities 'the nature of which is vital to the security of the state'. Given the open-ended nature of these terms and the degree of ministerial discretion involved, there must be a danger that politically partial judgments about who and what are legitimate security service targets are made.

# CHAPTER FOUR

# The Security Services Network

Each security and intelligence agency has its own formal structure, just like any other bureaucracy. But they also have formal and informal links with other organisations. The full extent of this network is hidden in Whitehall's subterranean world. The money the agencies spend is kept secret from both Parliament and the public, and their role is left deliberately vague. We shall look at each security service in turn.

## The constitutional position of MI5

The Security Service Act, which the Thatcher administration rushed through Parliament with the help of its large majority early in 1989, gives MI5 a statutory basis for the first time. It places MI5 under the authority of the Home Secretary. But throughout its history, and during the years following the second world war in particular, there was considerable confusion about its legal status and to whom it was responsible.

### *The Stewart Review 1945*

A review of MI5 undertaken by a senior civil servant, Sir Findlater Stewart, at the request of Sir Norman Brook, the Cabinet Secretary, stated: 'The purpose of the Security Service is the defence of the realm and nothing else. It follows that the minister responsible for it as a service should be the Minister of Defence.'[1]

Stewart noted that it had been argued that this would place 'an undue burden' on the minister. He appeared to reject this argument:

> From the very nature of the work the need for direction except on the very broadest lines can never arise above the level of Director-General. That appointment is one of great responsibility, calling for unusual experience and a rare combination of qualities; but having got the right man there is no alternative to giving him the widest discretion in the means he uses to, and the direction in which, he applies them – always provided he does not step outside the law.[2]

But the then Labour Prime Minister, Clement Attlee, was far from happy with Stewart's conclusions. He asked Brook to conduct a new review of the status of the Security Service.

## *The Brook Review 1951*

Brook said that Stewart had exaggerated the 'defence' aspects of the Security Service. In practice, he reported, MI5 had little to do with those aspects of the 'defence of the realm' with which the Ministry of Defence was concerned. According to Brook, MI5's functions were much more closely allied to those of the Home Office which had ultimate constitutional responsibility for 'defending the realm' against, as he put it, 'subversive activities' and for preserving law and order. Brook therefore recommended that the director-general of MI5 should be responsible to the home secretary; be able to turn to the permanent secretary at the Home Office 'for advice and assistance on the policy aspects of his work and on his relations with other government departments'; and see the prime minister 'on matters of supreme importance and delicacy'.[3]

The Brook Report and uneasiness about MI5's channels of responsibility within Whitehall led to the Maxwell-Fyfe Directive, named after the then Home Secretary. It has been the only official set of guidelines covering the activities of MI5 and it introduced a subtle change in the responsibilities of the agency and the government department to which it was nominally responsible.

## *The Maxwell-Fyfe Directive 1952*

The Directive advised that the director-general of the Security Service 'will be responsible to the Home Secretary personally'. It added: 'The Security Service is not, however, a part of the Home Office. On appropriate occasions you will have the right of direct access to the prime minister.' It urged the head of MI5 to take 'special care' to see that the work of the Security Service is 'strictly limited to what is necessary' for the purpose of its task. Its task was described by Maxwell-Fyfe as 'the defence of the realm as a whole' from espionage and sabotage 'or from actions of persons and organisations ... which may be judged to be subversive of the State'. The Directive also said it was 'essential' that the Security Service be kept 'absolutely free' from any political bias or influence.[4]

Although it had no legal status, the Directive used clearer and more specific language than the new Security Service Act nearly 40 years later. Even so, MI5 did not like it. In evidence to the Franks Committee set up by the Heath Government in 1972 to consider ways to reform the 1911 Official Secrets Act, Sir Martin Furnival-Jones, then MI5 Director-General, remarked that a directive was 'a very un-English thing.' He added: 'Certainly it is unusual in the government service for an organisation to be given a specific directive as to what its functions are, and what the limitations of its powers are.'[5]

The Maxwell-Fyfe Directive was not made public until 1963 when Lord Denning referred to it in his report on the Profumo affair.[6] It seemed that not even ministers were aware it. In the Commons debate on the Denning Report in 1963 the Prime Minister, Sir Alec Douglas-Home, said that the Directive 'illustrates how very easy it would be to cross the line between a free society and a police state'.[7] The Opposition leader, Harold Wilson, said that it had never occurred to prime ministers that their home secretaries were responsible for MI5. In *The Governance of Britain* (1976), Wilson said that the 1952 Directive and the home secretary's responsibility 'came as a complete surprise to members of parliament and the press, and apparently just as much of a surprise to No. 10'.[8]

## The Security Service Act 1989

It took a string of scandals and pressure for independent oversight in line with all of Britain's closest allies for the Government to accept the minimum it thought it could get away with – the appointment of a 'staff counsellor' for the security and intelligence services and the Security Service Act 1989 (see Appendix II).

Sir Philip Woodfield, a former Home Office official and Permanent Secretary of the Northern Ireland Office, was appointed to be the first 'staff counsellor'. Officials with problems – of conscience, for example – could go to him in confidence rather than to their immediate superiors. Sir Philip, who has refused invitations to discuss his role, operates part-time from the Cabinet Office, the very heart of the intelligence establishment he is supposed to hear complaints about. John Day, a former senior MI5 officer, has said of Woodfield's appointment: 'It ignores the real issues.'[9]

The Government decided to draw up the Act in the autumn of 1988 when it was caught in a case taken by *Liberty* to the European Commission of Human Rights. The Commission – whose task is to scrutinise applications to the Court itself – ruled that MI5 had a case to answer in two matters. Firstly, the surveillance of two former *Liberty* officers, Patricia Hewitt and Harriet Harman (now Labour MP for Peckham), and their classification as 'Communist sympathisers'. Secondly, the refusal of the defence contractor, MEL – a subsidiary of Philips electronics – to offer a job to a young accountant on the grounds of 'unsatisfactory' references – believed to be supplied by MI5. *Liberty* argued in part that Britain was contravening the European Convention on Human Rights because there was no 'effective remedy' against actions and complaints against MI5. Immediately after it published the Security Service Bill in November 1988, the Government sent a copy to the European Commission on Human Rights in an attempt to bring about a 'friendly settlement' in the case.

The Government's decision to place MI5 – but not MI6 or GCHQ – on a statutory basis for the first time in its 80-year history was announced in the Queen's Speech opening the new session of Parliament in November 1988. The

Bill was published the next day. By the following April, the measure had received the Royal Assent without a single amendment. But it did not come into force until December 18, 1989. The delay suggested that the Government's decision to push the measure through Parliament as quickly as possible earlier in the year was dictated by the desire to cut short an embarrassing and unwanted public debate about the security services rather than by any practical considerations.

## *Critique of the Act*

The Act does not cover the activities of Special Branch, GCHQ, or MI6 and it does not give Parliament any role in scrutinising the activities of MI5. The Act establishes a tribunal and commissioner to investigate complaints against MI5. However neither Parliament nor complainants will necessarily know what the tribunal or the commissioner discover during their investigations and their decisions cannot be challenged in the courts. Complainants will not have access to the files held on them by MI5. Even the successful complainant will not necessarily be told the nature of any unlawful surveillance or vetting, whether the tribunal has ordered that it must be stopped, or that any records held by MI5 are to be destroyed.

Where an individual complains that s/he has been vetted out of a job by MI5, the tribunal can only ask whether MI5 had 'reasonable grounds' for believing information disclosed to the prospective employer 'to be true'. The tribunal has no power to inquire why a particular post was subject to vetting procedures or to challenge MI5's definition and interpretation of 'subversion.' Neither can it question whether MI5 was justified in targeting a particular group of which the complainant was a member. It will be enough under the Act for MI5 to target an individual solely on the grounds that her or she is a member of a group deemed to be 'subversive'.

The Act gives complete discretion to the home secretary; there is no judicial control over MI5's administrative decisions. Although the Security Service commissioner – a senior judge – will monitor the issuing of warrants, this will only happen retrospectively and there is no one to monitor the judge's actions. The commissioner will work in secret and the annual report to the prime minister will be vetted for public consumption. The wording of the Act is vague and permissive. The emphasis throughout, when it describes the role of the tribunal or the home secretary, is on the word 'may' rather than 'shall'.

There are no limits on what MI5 can do under a warrant, and the employment-vetting role of MI5 is not subject to any firm statutory control or independent supervision. Neither the commissioner nor the tribunal will be able to scrutinise the data banks controlled by MI5.

The tribunal could investigate whether a warrant was wrongly authorised under the Act's broad criteria, or whether it was used wrongly – whether it was used for burgling, for example, when it referred only to bugging. But it is unlikely to be able to discover whether action by MI5 was illegal – that is, without any warrant at all. Thus, complainants will not know whether they have been the target of unauthorised action or whether the tribunal has determined (privately) that a warrant was properly authorised.

The procedures under the Security Service Act are modelled closely on those in the 1985 Interception of Communications Act covering mail-opening and telephone-tapping (see Chapter Six), also introduced as a result of a judgment against the Government under the European Convention on Human Rights.[10]

## MI5's role and structure

Altogether there are some 2,000 full-time MI5 officers with an annual budget of an estimated £200 millions. It is divided into a number of separate directorates or branches.

### *Intelligence resources and operations*

These are the responsibility of A Branch. They include investment in equipment such as the latest bugging devices and fieldwork like human surveillance and, on occasions, burglary, as well as the use of informers. A Branch co-ordinates MI5's contacts with other state agencies, including GCHQ, MI6 and Whitehall departments, as well as large companies and banks, publishing houses and the media.

A branch is divided up into a number of sections:

A1 – operations (including bugging and break-ins).
A2 – technical back-up, such as tapping devices.
A4 – watches, including vehicles.
A5 – scientific research.

### *Personnel*

B Branch is responsible for personnel, welfare issues, recruitment and vetting new staff as well as administration and internal finance. From the post-war period through to the 1960s, MI5 attracted ex-police officers, armed forces personnel and former officials from the diminishing colonial service. More recently, it has sought to overcome the agency's recruitment problem by asking a private consultancy firm to draw up advertisements – aimed at university graduates – couched in suitably disguised terms. It has also strengthened its

legal department. MI5's personnel department was savagely criticised in a report by the Security Commission in 1985 concerning the events which led to the arrest of Michael Bettaney, a young MI5 officer, who, as we have seen, passed sensitive information to the Soviet embassy in London.
B Branch is also divided up into a number of sections:

B1 – recruitment.

B2 – personnel management.

B3 – general management services.

B5 – finance.

## *Protective security*

C Branch is responsible for 'protective security', including advising Whitehall on how to secure government buildings and prevent leaks of information. C Branch draws up contingency plans for emergencies and conducts exercises with the SAS and special police units. These operations are intended to prepare for hypothetical crises such as the occupation of a nuclear power station.

C Branch assists Whitehall departments and Scotland Yard's serious crime squad during leak inquiries. It also helps Ministry of Defence investigators responsible for carrying out vetting inquiries. The Branch will in turn check records on individuals held by F Branch.

C Branch is divided as follows:

C1 – security in Whitehall.

C2 – the vetting of government contractors.

C3 – the vetting of civil servants.

C4 – security against potential terrorist attacks.

## *Domestic surveillance*

F Branch is in charge of monitoring the activities of those individuals or groups whom MI5 considers 'subversive.' It has been the most controversial directorate within MI5. As the former MI5 officer, Miranda Ingram, put it: 'Working here means monitoring one's fellow-citizens.'[11] It expanded rapidly during the 1970s. Insiders now claim less attention is paid to political and campaigning groups with no record of violence and more to terrorist groups.

F Branch is divided up into different sections, each responsible for specific targets:

F1 – the Communist Party (CPGB).

F2 – trade unions (in the public sector as well as in private industry).

F3 – non-Irish terrorism.
F4 – agents in the CPGB and trade unions.
F5 – Irish terrorism.
F6 – agents in radical groups and terrorist organisations.
F7 – political, radical and campaigning groups, which have included nationalists, pacifists, MPs, teachers, lawyers, journalists, the Campaign for Nuclear Disarmament (CND), the National Council for Civil Liberties (*Liberty*), and the Anti-Blood Sports League.

Overall control of the running of agents and handling informers, including those within the media and publishing houses, comes under a section called FX.

The present Director-General of MI5, Patrick Walker, who was appointed at the end of 1987, was previously head of F Branch and had earlier worked in F5.

## *Counter-intelligence*

K Branch is responsible for counter-espionage operations; that is to say, countering the activities of hostile intelligence services in Britain. It is divided up in the following way:

K1 – monitors potential penetration of Whitehall departments.
K2 – monitors the KGB and GRU (the Soviet military intelligence).
K3 – recruitment of Soviet agents.
K4 – surveillance of Soviet diplomats, trade delegations, etc.
K5 – recruitment of Eastern European and Chinese agents.
K6 – recruitment of other 'hostile' intelligence agents in Britain.
K7 – investigates possible penetration of British security and intelligence agencies, including MI5 itself.
K8 – non-Soviet-bloc counter-intelligence.

As we shall see in greater detail in Chapter Six, in the 1960s Security Service officers in K5, with officials drafted in from MI6, monitored and bugged the associates of Harold Wilson, allegedly with the authority of the then heads of MI5 and MI6.[12]

## *Training and computer files*

S Branch is responsible for training MI5 officers and MI5's registry and computer centre. MI5 was slow to introduce computers, partly because of the inherent conservatism of its senior management, partly because of concern about the vulnerability of computers to hacking. (Senior MI5 officers were also worried about the possibility of outsiders 'reading' computers through the 'radiation' they emit.)

S Branch is also divided into sections:

S1 – runs the Joint Computer Bureau linked to other agencies, including MI6.

S2 – the registry of files.

S3 – training.

S4 – supplies travel arrangements, etc.

MI5's computing facility is based on a powerful twin ICL 2980 system with a capacity of 20 million separate files. Actual files on individuals number about one million. This central computer is linked to a national network of smaller computers and access terminals set up by MI5.

## The constitutional position of the Special Branch

The Security Service Act makes no mention of the Special Branch (SB). During the debates on the Act in Parliament, the Government argued that SB officers were accountable in the same way as the rest of the police. The implication was that the Special Branch is politically accountable through the chief constable to the local police authorities, and in the case of the Metropolitan Police, to the home secretary. In practice, chief constables enjoy wide discretionary powers. Police authorities have little or no control over the operations and expenditure of the local force. Home secretaries refuse to answer questions from MPs on police operations, although under Section 3 of the Police Act 1964, they have the power to require a report on any matter from a chief constable (although how much they ask, and have the time to digest, is questionable). 'The real paradox', according to one writer, 'is that at the moment he [the Home Secretary] has a statutory right to be informed but does not have to pass the information on to Parliament.'[13]

In 1985, in a memorandum to the inquiry on the Special Branch by the Commons Home Affairs Committee, John Alderson, the former Chief Constable of Devon and Cornwall, described the role of the SB in these terms:

> The SB in a police force (Metropolitan Police excepted) is a relatively small branch of the CID. It is answerable to the head of the CID and through him to an assistant chief constable and ultimately to the chief constable. The terms of reference drawn up by the Home Office in consultation with the Association of Chief Police officers and the security service are concerned with the monitoring and control of

> subversion and the monitoring of threats to public order. Both the Metropolitan Police and the security service pass to and receive from provincial police forces information concerning joint or national interest. Since the security services have no police powers, and also wish to retain their anonymity, the Special Branch undertakes overt action in criminal cases.[14]

## Special Branch's role and structure

MI5 has no official executive authority – it does not 'execute' the political decisions of ministers in the way conventional civil servants do. It is like the police in that its main role is investigatory. But unlike the police it has no power of arrest. This role is fulfilled by the Special Branch, sometimes referred to as MI5's eyes and ears, sometimes as their footsoldiers.

In the 1950s, the Special Branch totalled about 200 officers. But the number increased significantly during the late 1960s and early 1970s – a time of widespread political protest and industrial unrest – and by 1975 every local police force had its own Special Branch under the control of the local chief constable. There are now over 2,000 SB officers, with about 450 based in London and a total annual budget of about £20 millions. The size of SB units in different parts of the country varies, depending, for example, on the number of ports and airports in the area. Asked in March 1988 by the Labour MP, Ken Livingstone, to give the number of Special Branch officers in the Royal Ulster Constabulary, John Stanley, then Northern Ireland Minister responsible for security, replied: 'In the particular operational circumstances of Northern Ireland this information is confidential.'[15]

A Special Branch central index has the names and 'areas of interest' of an estimated 2 million individuals stored on Scotland Yard's C Department computer.

## Special Branch guidelines

In 1984, following growing controversy over its activities, the Home Office published new guidelines for the Special Branch (see Appendix III). The guidelines make it clear that the Special Branch is an integral part of the country's security and intelligence-gathering apparatus. Indeed, the Met SB, rather than MI5, has been at the forefront of the fight against terrorism. MI5 has been slow to shift its attention and resources to anti-terrorism, preferring to concentrate on its traditional task of countering Communist bloc activities in Britain and on domestic 'subversion'.

A National Joint Unit at Scotland Yard co-ordinates information and enquiries when a local Special Branch arrests or questions individuals under the Prevention of Terrorism Act.

Its guidelines give the Special Branch a great deal of discretion. They state, for example, that the SB 'gathers information about threats to public order'. They also state that 'care should be taken to ensure that only necessary and relevant information is recorded and retained. Each Special Branch should therefore maintain an effective system both for updating information where necessary and for weeding out and destroying information which can no longer be clearly related to the discharge of its functions.' Again, the practice is different from the theory. Police, says Alderson, want two things: 'more power and more information'. Of their thirst for information, he says, 'they can't get enough of it.' To take an example, activists involved in the campaign against the South African rugby tour during the winter of 1969/70 were investigated. Ten years later, their movements were still being recorded. The file on one citizen in Devon noted that he had had 'lunch with Wedgwood Benn'.[16]

Asked by the Labour MP, Clare Short, roughly how many files the SB kept on individuals, the then head of Scotland Yard's Special Branch, Deputy Assistant Commissioner Hewitt, told the Commons Home Affairs Committee: 'I do not think it is in the public interest to give the number of records that we keep.'[17]

When he was Chief Constable of Devon and Cornwall, Alderson took the initiative to weed out what he regarded as superfluous SB files. He told BBC Radio's 'File on Four' in August 1982:

> When I looked at my records, I came to the conclusion that there were items of intelligence in there that should never be in: I mean, one could make a case out for including a file on everyone who protests, because of one kind or another. I mean, some people will go so far as to say that the League Against Cruel Sports is a threat to liberties ... the anti nuclear movement has very great difficulties in this connection in expressing its views without being regarded as subversive. So, looking at my records, I came to the conclusion that getting on for 50 percent of them should never have been in there, either because they were a waste of time and clogging up the machine, or they were records of activities which shouldn't be in those banks of information.[18]

The 50 percent coincides with estimates of the proportion of SB officers who are concerned not with terrorism or the protection of individuals, but with 'political' targets, including trade union activists involved in industrial action. Alderson told the Commons Home Affairs Committee that in industrial disputes 'the Special Branch have to report daily on the number of pickets ... a daily report on all industrial disputes is sent to police headquarters and in appropriate cases to the Home Office.'[19] What he did not realise was that though he was constitutionally the head of his Special Branch, some of the files he ordered to be weeded were sent to MI5 in London. One Special Branch file which was not closed was that of Hugh Geach, a former social worker and Oxfam employee, and an SDP candidate in local elections. The file on Geach was opened when, as a student at Reading University, he was one of the leaders of the 1970 campaign against the South African rugby tour. Although no new information had appeared on his file since 1972, it had still not been weeded out ten years later.[20]

## MI5 – Special Branch links

The Special Branch guidelines openly acknowledge the close links between the two agencies. 'A Special Branch', they say, 'assists the Security Service in carrying out its tasks of defending the realm against attempts at espionage and sabotage or from the actions of persons and organisations whether directed from within or without the country which may be judged subversive to the State.'[21] Many of the names on MI5's central files were originally provided by local SB forces.

In each of its nine regions MI5 has a senior officer – often a retired assistant commissioner of the local force who was responsible for the Special Branch in the area – to work with a police liaison officer. His or her job is to ensure that the chief constable provides adequate facilities for the SB and sanctions instructions it receives from MI5. Persuasion will, however, come from higher levels where this proves necessary for MI5 to obtain what it wants, such as information on targets and help in surveillance.

In the mid 1970s, the Chief Constable of Strathclyde hesitated when faced with an MI5 request for his men to break into the Glasgow offices of the Communist Party. In the end, the Director-General of MI5 personally persuaded him to undertake the operation.

Sometimes, MI5 and the SB share the workload. For example, when the security officer of a company wants information on members of its workforce, he or she would normally get in touch with the SB rather than with MI5. The SB would contact MI5 if it wanted more, or different, information. On other occasions, MI5 would itself ask the security officer about 'subversives' in a company and would even send in its own agents, as it did with British Leyland in the early 1980s (see Chapter Five).

It is normal practice for MI5 to bypass the local chief constable, dealing directly with the local Special Branch. In the end, according to John Alderson, a chief constable 'can't do anything about MI5; nobody can do anything about it'.[22]

## The constitutional position of MI6

The Government continues to maintain the fiction that MI6 does not officially exist in peacetime though similar agencies in all other western democracies are openly acknowledged. In February 1988, the Tory MP, Richard Shepherd, asked the Foreign Secretary whether he would issue a directive to the head of MI6 along the lines of the Maxwell-Fyfe Directive which had theoretically governed MI5's activities since 1952. 'It has been the long-established practice', David Mellor, the Foreign Office Minister of State replied, 'of this and previous governments not to comment on such matters'.[23]

## MI6's role

While MI5 operates at home and in the colonies, the Secret Intelligence Service, commonly called MI6, mainly operates abroad. That is the general rule, though it has come apart in Northern Ireland where the two agencies have clashed over policy and methods. MI6 has a London station where, like MI5, it is also involved in counter-intelligence. Traditional rivalry between MI6 and MI5 – the former regarding themselves as the gentlemen, the latter the players – is slowly being replaced by co-operation, notably in the fight against terrorism. However, tension remains and there is a culture gap between the two agencies: MI6 tends to look ahead at the longer term and is less isolated than its MI5 counterpart.

MI6 works closely with the Foreign Office – most of its agents operate from British embassies and high commissions abroad under diplomatic cover. But their reports go to the Joint Intelligence Organisation, which is part of the Cabinet Office (see Chapter Five). In the past few years, MI6 has given way to GCHQ, as ministers and the Cabinet Office have relied increasingly on signals intelligence (SIGINT). But recently SIGINT has not contributed significantly to intelligence about Eastern Europe or the Middle East. And on occasions, MI6 advice has been ignored. Neglect of the kind of traditional intelligence-gathering that is MI6's stock in trade contributed to the failure of the Government to foresee the Argentine invasion of the Falklands in 1982. The MI6 Head of Station in Buenos Aires, the agency's last remaining post in South America, gave London ample warnings about a possible attack on the islands. And in another example, MI6 agents in Salisbury, capital of what was then Rhodesia, told the Wilson Government in vain that, if British forces were sent out quickly in the aftermath of the country's unilateral declaration of independence from Britain, few Rhodesian soldiers or airmen would fight their 'kith and kin'. This view has since been supported by Ken Flower, the head of Ian Smith's secret service.[24]

Fast-moving events in Europe in 1989 enabled MI6 to argue that it should be given a new priority as traditional assumptions about a divided Germany, and the continuing presence of US troops in West Germany, are being challenged. Less certain is how ministers and their advisers in Whitehall will act on MI6 reports and their implicit call for a radical rethink of British policy towards Europe.

## MI6's structure

MI6 is estimated to have a budget of about £160 millions a year and a staff of about 3,000. The present Chief of MI6 – or 'C' as he is still known within Whitehall – is Sir Colin McColl, appointed by Margaret Thatcher in January 1989.

After the second world war MI6 divided the world into four main areas, each under a number of directors of production:

- DP1 – covers Europe. There is a Controller for the Northern Area (P1) covering the Soviet Union and Scandinavia; Controller for the Western Area (P2) responsible for France, Spain, and North Africa; Controller for the Eastern Area (P3) covering Germany, Austria and Switzerland.
- DP2 – under the Controller, the Middle East (called P4).
- DP3 – under the Controller, Far East (P5) which also covers South America.
- DP4 – is responsible for London-based operations.

There are nine 'Directors of Requirements', responsible for the following sections: political affairs, air, naval, military, counter-intelligence, economic, financial, GCHQ, and scientific.[25]

## The constitutional position of GCHQ

There are no official charters or guidelines governing the Government Communications Headquarters (GCHQ) based at Cheltenham. GCHQ is not covered by the 1989 Security Service Act, although some of its operations are effectively sanctioned by the Interception of Communications Act without actually mentioning GCHQ by name (or any other security agency).

To the dismay – and apparent surprise – of ministers, GCHQ became a household name as a result of the bitter controversy surrounding Thatcher's decision, announced on January 25, 1984, to ban all staff from membership of a trade union. GCHQ's role was first officially 'avowed' in 1982 after the arrest of Geoffrey Prime, a Russian linguist at GCHQ who, as we have seen, had been spying for the Soviet Union for at least nine years, between 1968 and 1977. The full extent of GCHQ's activities first came to light during the ABC secrets trial in 1978 when two journalists, Duncan Campbell and Crispin Aubrey, and a former soldier, John Berry, were charged with disclosing information about Britain's secret electronic eavesdropping network.[26]

For many years international cables have been recorded by intelligence agencies. As technology developed, so did the extent of eavesdropping on diplomatic, commercial, and private communications. Now satellites and monitoring equipment linked to GCHQ have the capacity to 'harvest' all international telephone communications, as well as domestic ones.

There is no outside body monitoring GCHQ's activities. The only safeguard is the entirely voluntary action of the officials responsible for collecting and storing intercepted communications. To take an entirely realistic example: a man with an Irish name, say Patrick, telephones a friend in Chicago who also has an Irish name, Sean. Their conversation is monitored and their names arouse suspicion – it is an entirely private conversation but GCHQ argues that the two men could be discussing ways of getting money, or even arms, to Northern Ireland. What happens to the recorded tape? A benevolent official may destroy the record, a malevolent one keeps it and passes it on to officials in the Joint Intelligence Organisation at the Cabinet Office in London. One thing, however, is clear – whatever decision is made, the conversation is listened to.

## GCHQ's role

GCHQ is in theory sponsored by the Foreign Office. Its staff, like that of MI6, is attached to British embassies and high commissions abroad. It intercepts communications of foreign countries and operates closely with the US. However, most of its budget is supplied by the Ministry of Defence and it is increasingly involved in monitoring domestic communications. GCHQ's targets, including individuals, groups and companies, are automatically intercepted. They include foreign oil companies, banks, newspapers, commodity dealers, radical political or civil rights groups as well as foreign embassies and suspected terrorists. Computer systems are being developed and programmed to look for key words and to recognise voices to help GCHQ monitors to cope with the enormous bureaucratic task of transcribing so much material. The more complex the task the greater the risk to innocent people.

The functions of GCHQ are described in its official recruitment advertisements as responsibility 'for ensuring the security of British official and military communications' and developing 'cryptographic equipment and systems to protect these'. GCHQ, the official literature euphemistically adds, 'studies foreign communications and electronic emissions as directed by ministers for defence and foreign intelligence purposes'.

Part of GCHQ's work is protective – developing scrambling systems, for example, to safeguard British secret and coded diplomatic and military communications. But one of its main tasks now is to intercept, and as far as possible interpret and analyse, the communications of others – not only the military and diplomatic traffic of potentially hostile powers, but the communications of friendly countries, companies and private individuals. Such use of advanced computers – hoovering of the air-waves – is frequently described as 'technotyranny'.

GCHQ is part of a worldwide secret SIGINT network initially set up by Britain and the US in the 1946 UKUSA Treaty which other countries – Canada, Australia and New Zealand – later joined as secondary partners. They divided up the world between them, listening to traffic through radio receivers, intercepting microwave or ground telephone communications, and receiving information from US reconnaissance or eavesdropping satellites. GCHQ, for example, sends the US information picked up by its listening posts at Ayios Nikolaos in Cyprus or Hong Kong and receives in return the results of intelligence gathered by US satellites. Australia receives intelligence information from the US in return for hosting the US satellite base at Pine Gap.

Other countries with stations in the SIGINT chain are West Germany, Denmark, Norway, Japan and South Korea.

## GCHQ's structure

Some 7,000 civil servants – mathematicians, linguists, computer programmers and engineers, cypher clerks, radio operators, and codebreakers – work at GCHQ. In addition, about 4,000 army and RAF signals specialists are attached to GCHQ, based mainly at the agency's outstations. Its annual budget is estimated at between £260 and £750 millions. The present GCHQ Director is John Adye.

GCHQ has two main directorates. The directorate of Organisation and Establishment is subdivided into a number of divisions:

C – responsible for overseas staff.
E – personnel.
F – finance and supply.
G – management and general.
M – mechanical engineering.
Q – technical.
R – security.

The directorate of SIGINT operations and requirements is divided into the following divisions:

H – cryptanalysis.

J – special SIGINT.
K – general SIGINT.
S/T – statistical operations.
U/V – search technology.
W – communications.
X – computer services.
Z – liaison.

GCHQ also has a chief scientist, a director of communications, a directorate of communications security, a directorate of SIGINT plans, and a director of plans and policy staff.

A special unit has recently been set up to monitor the telephone calls and activities of radical groups and individuals within Britain that are considered 'subversive'. Called K20, it collects transcribed tapes and passes the information on to officials in the Joint Intelligence Committee based in the Cabinet Office in London. The operation is a reflection of how GCHQ, with the vast technical resources at its disposal, is expanding its empire in the intelligence world and is taking on some of the operations traditionally undertaken by MI5.

## The union ban

The ban preventing GCHQ staff from being members of an independent trade union – which until then they had been officially encouraged to join – was imposed by the Government in 1984. The ban was opposed by senior civil servants, the International Labour Organisation, and by a very small number of Tory MPs (notably John Gorst), who were prepared to voice their belief in the right to belong to a trade union as well as the right not to do so. The ban, however, was supported by the European Court of Human Rights which was not prepared to challenge the Government's argument that it was necessary in the interest of 'national security'.

That argument was introduced by the Government only after the High Court had ruled that the decision was invalid because of the way it had been introduced, without any consultation with the staff involved. The Prime Minister told Civil Service union leaders after the ban that there was 'an inherent conflict of loyalties' between membership of a national trade union and the defence of 'national security'. She said that the gap between her position and that of the unions 'could not be bridged by words' – in effect, she was saying she could not, or would not, explain her decision.[27]

What is certain is that the consequences of the ban were considerably more disruptive than previous industrial actions at GCHQ. Many skilled computer staff – already in short supply at GCHQ – left to take up more lucrative employment in private companies where unions were not banned. Mike

Grindley, GCHQ's sole mandarin Chinese linguist, was sacked after refusing to give up his union membership. Other valuable staff left in protest, including Alexander Hamilton, a brilliant cryptanalyst renowned on both sides of the Atlantic and who has given his name to code-breaking methods.

Dennis Mitchell also left GCHQ in protest against the ban. For 32 years he had worked as a cryptanalyst in one of the most sensitive areas of the agency's work. In January 1987 Mitchell told senior MPs that he had 'arrived at the point at which I either make my concerns public, which means breaking the Official Secrets Act, or I fail to discharge my responsibility to account for actions which I believe would be considered unacceptable by the general public were it aware of them.'[28] Sir Robert Armstrong, the Cabinet Secretary, ordered government lawyers to go immediately to the High Court to get an injunction preventing Mitchell from disclosing anything about his work at GCHQ. Though his conscience remains troubled, he also remains bound by the court injunction.

In an article in *The Guardian* to which Armstrong said he had no objection, Mitchell wrote:

> GCHQ is an industrial complex. Its product is intelligence. Intelligence imparts power; power which may be used to withstand a threat – or to apply one; to avert an ill, to bestow a benefit – or to exploit. Intelligence shared is power shared; intelligence withheld confers power over the unaware. GCHQ provides power to the British Government; and governments with which it is allied. GCHQ staff have a moral responsibility, both corporate and individual, for the use to which that power is put. The human instruments of the Nazi regime stood condemned at Nuremburg because they shirked their moral responsibility.

Mitchell described GCHQ as a powerful, but unaccountable, arm of government. The only watchdog is the workforce. 'It is they', he said, 'on whom the general public must rely if errors of judgment, excessive zeal or malpractices are to be averted in a department which has considerable discretion and no outside inspection.'[29]

The effect of the union ban, Mitchell argued, is that the workforce is now less likely to be representative of the population as a whole. It will be distorted, people with strong regard for civil liberties are less likely to work there, resulting in a GCHQ with more than its natural share of 'yes-men'.

Only about 100 of GCHQ's 7,000 civilian staff refused to accept the March 1, 1985 deadline for leaving their union – a figure which bore out Dennis Mitchell's concerns.

## GCHQ and South Africa

GCHQ continues to play an important part in Britain's continuing intelligence links with South Africa. The eavesdropping station at Silvermine, close to the Simonstown naval base, passes on information to Cheltenham. GCHQ and the National Security Agency (NSA), its US counterpart, are reported to have provided information to the South African government about the activities and movements of Pretoria's political opponents.[30] In return, Pretoria was asked to continue providing the US and Britain with information about Soviet and Cuban activities in Angola as well as Russian shipping movements around the Cape. The *New York Times* reported in July 1986 that British and American officials discussed the operation at a regular review of intelligence assignments – called 'tasking' – at GCHQ headquarters in Cheltenham in the mid-1980s. Seymour Hersh, the respected US journalist, said his source – a former NSA official – described how at one point 'three South African military intelligence officers were ushered into the room'. The participants then exchanged requirements. The former NSA official said that the South African list included intercepting the communications of the Angola, Mozambique, Zambia and Botswana governments and information relating to the ANC, including the movements of its leader, Oliver Tambo. The CIA and the US State Department denied the story.[31]

It is known, however, that GCHQ has facilities at the British High Commission in Lusaka, the Zambian capital, and that both the CIA and British intelligence have enjoyed good relations with South Africa's National Intelligence Organisation, previously called BOSS, the Bureau of State Security. Gordon Winter, one-time BOSS agent, said in his book, *Inside BOSS*, that MI5 provided South Africa with information about British left-wingers in the mid-1960s.[32]

## GCHQ and NSA

But of all the links between western intelligence agencies, those between GCHQ and the NSA based at Fort Meade, Maryland, are the closest. The US makes direct contributions to GCHQ on top of the expenditure paid for by the British taxpayer. In the late 1960s, the US persuaded Britain – through senior GCHQ officials – to install listening posts at the GCHQ base in Morwenstow, north Cornwall. Morwenstow is only about 50 miles from British Telecom's site at Goonhilly Down, its Intelsat ground station for transatlantic traffic, close to where the main transatlantic cable comes ashore and where communications are relayed to the rest of Britain and Europe by microwave. The NSA has listening stations at Chicksands, Bedfordshire, and Edzell on Tayside. The NSA and GCHQ jointly operate two overseas stations – on Ascension Island and on Diego Garcia in the Indian Ocean.

But the most important NSA station is at Menwith Hill, near Harrogate in Yorkshire. Menwith Hill has been described as the biggest tapping centre in the world. It has the capacity to monitor 20,000 circuits simultaneously and the potential to monitor a quarter of a million domestic telephone lines within Britain.

In the late 1960s, the US Government approved a project, code-named Minaret, authorising NSA's eavesdropping on the international communications of a watch list of civil rights and anti-Vietnam campaigners. They included the actress, Jane Fonda, the singer Joan Baez and the celebrated baby-book author, Benjamin Spock.

Minaret was discovered by the US Senate's Church Committee set up in the wake of Watergate.[33] The committee concluded that NSA's 'potential to violate the privacy of American citizens is unmatched by any other intelligence agency.' That applies equally to GCHQ. Indeed, the Minaret operation – with private communications intercepted at Morwenstow and Menwith Hill – could not have operated without at least the passive co-operation of GCHQ. By intercepting the calls in Britain, NSA avoided breaking the letter of US legislation, notably the Federal Communications Act. By the same token, NSA listens to the conversations of British citizens and passes information on to the British Government.

# CHAPTER FIVE

## How the Security Network Links Up

The security and intelligence agencies link and co-operate in a network of official committees with the prime minister at the nexus (see diagrams pp60-63). These committees, however, do not reveal the full picture. Petty jealousies and rivalries common to any bureaucratic system have bedevilled relationships between the different agencies. Different prime ministers have had different priorities, instincts and suspicions. The former Labour Prime Minister, Harold Wilson, preferred to deal with MI6 than MI5, whom he did not trust, while Margaret Thatcher favours MI5. Both the agencies and committees have unacknowledged links with other parts of the government machine. MI5, for example, has a 'plant' in the Bank of England. The agencies also have informal links with merchant bankers and businessmen. In addition, the growth of private security companies with unofficial links to government agencies presents the spectre of a parallel security and intelligence network, the implications of which have hardly begun to be realised.

### Official committees

The Permanent Secretaries Committee on the Intelligence Services (PSIS) is chaired by the Cabinet Secretary – currently Sir Robin Butler. Its other members are the permanent secretaries of the Foreign Office, the Home Office, the Treasury, and the Chief of Defence Staff. It discusses general priorities, potential political embarrassments or scandals, and the budgets of the security and intelligence agencies. It reports to the prime minister but it is not concerned with operations.

Raw intelligence – that is, the reports of agents in the field, of tapped telephone conversations, of eavesdropping by GCHQ – is channelled to the Joint Intelligence Organisation (JIO). The JIO, which is part of the Cabinet Office, consists of assessment staff who draw up daily reports as well as long-term analyses. It is divided into Current Intelligence Groups (CIGs) assigned to different geographical areas – Latin America, for example. A special CIG has been set up specifically to concentrate on potential terrorist threats.

The JIO sends information to the Joint Intelligence Committee (JIC), a group of officials who are the central filter between expert assessors and ministers. The JIC has two offshoots based abroad. JIC (G) is based in Bonn and is chaired by the local MI6 station officer. Its task is to monitor political and economic developments in Central and Eastern Europe but it has also been concerned with IRA terrorist activities on the continent, and in particular with attacks on British military personnel and their families. It liaises with the British Services Security Organisation (BSSO).[1] JIC (C) is based in Cyprus, which remains an important listening post monitoring both military and political developments in the Middle East.

The JIC in London is chaired by Sir Percy Cradock, officially described as the Prime Minister's foreign policy adviser and a former ambassador to China. Its members include the heads of MI5, MI6, and GCHQ, the deputy chief of defence staff responsible for intelligence and the chair and deputy of the JIO assessment staff. Representatives of the US, Canadian, Australian and New Zealand governments also participate when items of international interest are on the agenda. Every Wednesday JIO staff draw up summary assessments, contained in weekly surveys of intelligence, commonly called 'red books' or 'wizard'. The JIC considers them on Thursdays. Its full, unexpurgated, reports are then sent to selected ministers – the prime minister, the defence secretary, the home secretary, the foreign secretary, the chancellor – and also to the Queen. MI5 reports are distributed separately in 'blue books'. GCHQ reports and transcribed tapes are delivered daily to the Cabinet Office. The Northern Ireland secretary also sees relevant intelligence reports. The chancellor is additionally a member of the Ministerial Committee on Intelligence (MIS) which fixes budget priorities on the basis of briefs prepared by the PSIS.

The co-ordinator of intelligence and security is currently Sir Christopher Curwen, a former head of MI6. He reports directly to the Prime Minister and as his title suggests is primarily responsible for trying to ensure that the different agencies work with each other in the most effective way. His job, as well as that of the JIC, which he attends, have been helped by the construction of a new communications centre beneath Whitehall to speed up the collection of information from sources and agencies outside London.

Other, more specialist, agencies and committees include:

- The Defence Intelligence Staff (DIS), with a staff of about 700. It supplies threat assessments, principally of Warsaw Pact countries. It uses a wide range of remote sensing and surveillance technologies, backed up by military attachés posted to British missions overseas. It also uses material provided by signals intelligence (SIGINT) supplied by GCHQ and the US National Security Agency and by co-operation with other NATO countries. DIS is influential in determining defence commitments, and has a reputation for providing 'worst case' assessments of the Soviet threat. For example, it greatly exaggerated the size and effectiveness of Soviet forces in Afghanistan.

- The London Signals Intelligence Board (LSIB), with officials from GCHQ, DIS and MI6, monitors GCHQ's work.

- The Overseas Economic Intelligence Committee (OEIC) is chaired by Treasury officials and includes civil servants from the Department of Trade and Industry, the Department of Energy, the Foreign Office, the Ministry of Defence and GCHQ.

- A number of committees deal with security within Whitehall such as positive vetting, leak inquiries, the classification of documents, the physical security of government buildings and the protection of sensitive information held on computers. They include the Official Committee on Security and the Personnel Security Committee – both chaired by the Cabinet Secretary – the Security Policy and Methods Committee and the Electronic Security Committee.

Other agencies which should be included as part of the security and intelligence apparatus are:

- The Ministry of Defence (MoD) police, with about 4,000 officers under its own chief constable. Demonstrations against nuclear bases – both British and American (where Britain is responsible for civil order) – have increased its workload, and have sometimes caused tensions with the local police. The MoD police is responsible for the bases but does not have jurisdiction outside. RAF nuclear weapons stores are guarded by the separate (armed) RAF police.

- The UK Atomic Energy Authority Constabulary has about 650 armed officers. They were originally restricted to within a 15-mile radius of nuclear installations. The Constabulary, which is responsible to the Department of Energy, can now operate anywhere.

- The Post Office Investigation Department, many of whose staff are former policemen, has as its main function the prevention of crime within major sorting offices. One of its tasks is to intercept and open mail on instructions from MI5.

## Co-ordinator of Intelligence & Security

The Co-ordinator, Sir Christopher Curwen, formerly chief of SIS (MI6), advises the Prime Minister on security and intelligence matters and has an office serviced by members of the Joint Intelligence staff.

## Joint Intelligence Committee

Together with its Joint Intelligence Organisation, this constitutes a central part of the intelligence assessment process. It is chaired by Sir Percy Cradock, a former ambassador.
The committee meets weekly to review assessments made by the JIO and forward them to the Prime Minister and Cabinet. Staff of the agencies in the UKUSA Agreement countries (US, Canada, Australia and New Zealand) participate in some meetings.

## Overseas Economic Intelligence Committee

Chaired by a Treasury official and includes representatives from the Department of Trade and Industry, Foreign Office and Department of Energy, together with the heads of GCHQ, DIS and SIS.

## London Signals Intelligence Board

Created in 1942, this monitors the work of GCHQ. It includes the heads of GCHQ, DIS and SIS as well as the director of the Government Code & Cypher School.

## London Signals Intelligence Committee (Defence)

Sub-committee of LSIB concerned with military signals.

## Joint Intelligence Organisation

Based in the Cabinet Office, its function is to prepare assessments on a wide range of external situations and it also has a co-ordinating function for intelligence and security activities. Its staff are seconded to the Cabinet Office, principally from the Foreign Office and Ministry of Defence.

## GCHQ

Government Communications Headquarters
(see overleaf)

## DIS

Defence Intelligence Staff

(see overleaf)

## SIS (MI6)

(see overleaf)

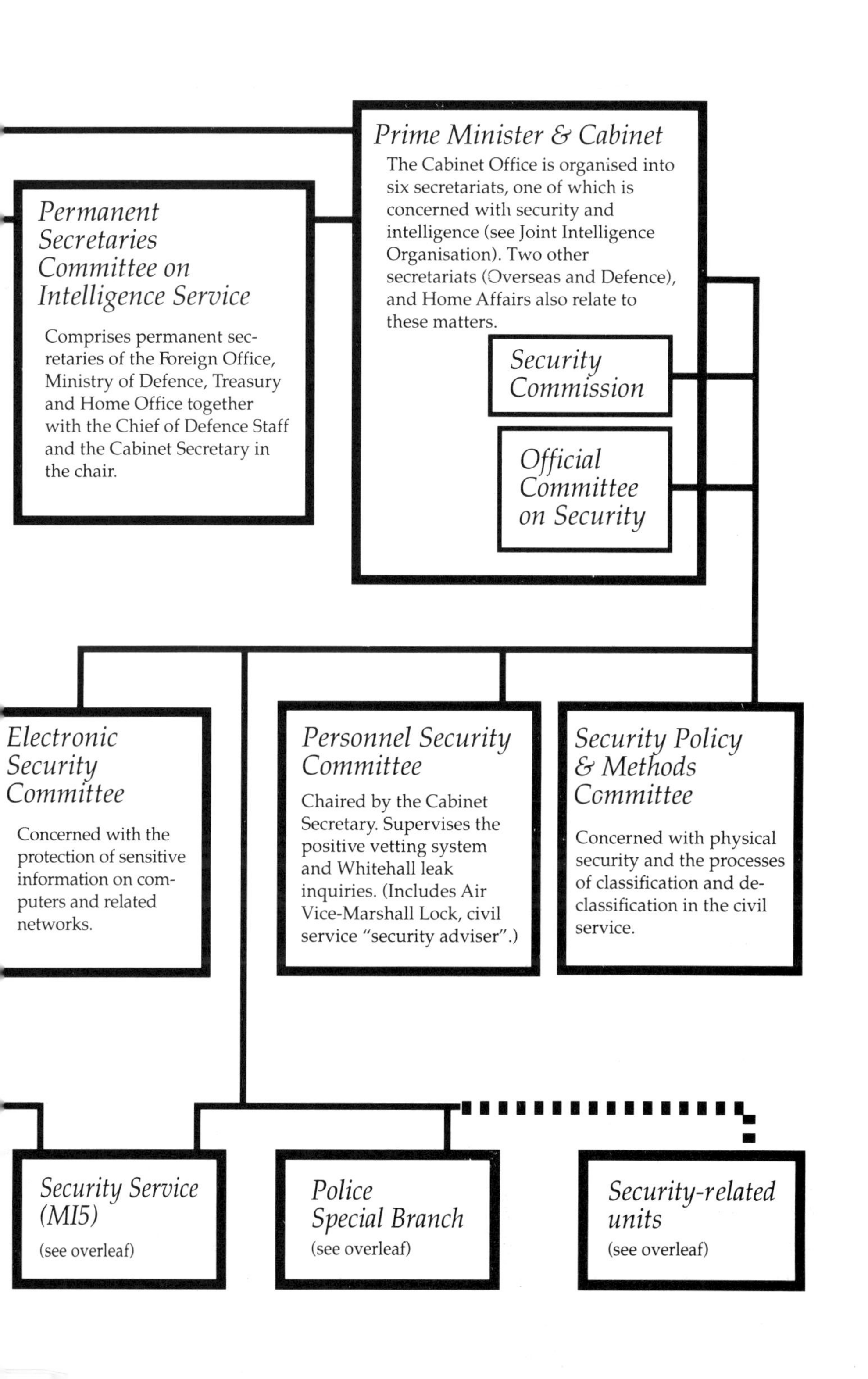
Prime Minister & Cabinet
The Cabinet Office is organised into six secretariats, one of which is concerned with security and intelligence (see Joint Intelligence Organisation). Two other secretariats (Overseas and Defence), and Home Affairs also relate to these matters.
Security Commission
Official Committee on Security
Permanent Secretaries Committee on Intelligence Service
Comprises permanent secretaries of the Foreign Office, Ministry of Defence, Treasury and Home Office together with the Chief of Defence Staff and the Cabinet Secretary in the chair.
Electronic Security Committee
Concerned with the protection of sensitive information on computers and related networks.
Personnel Security Committee
Chaired by the Cabinet Secretary. Supervises the positive vetting system and Whitehall leak inquiries. (Includes Air Vice-Marshall Lock, civil service "security adviser".)
Security Policy & Methods Committee
Concerned with physical security and the processes of classification and declassification in the civil service.
Security Service (MI5)
(see overleaf)
Police Special Branch
(see overleaf)
Security-related units
(see overleaf)

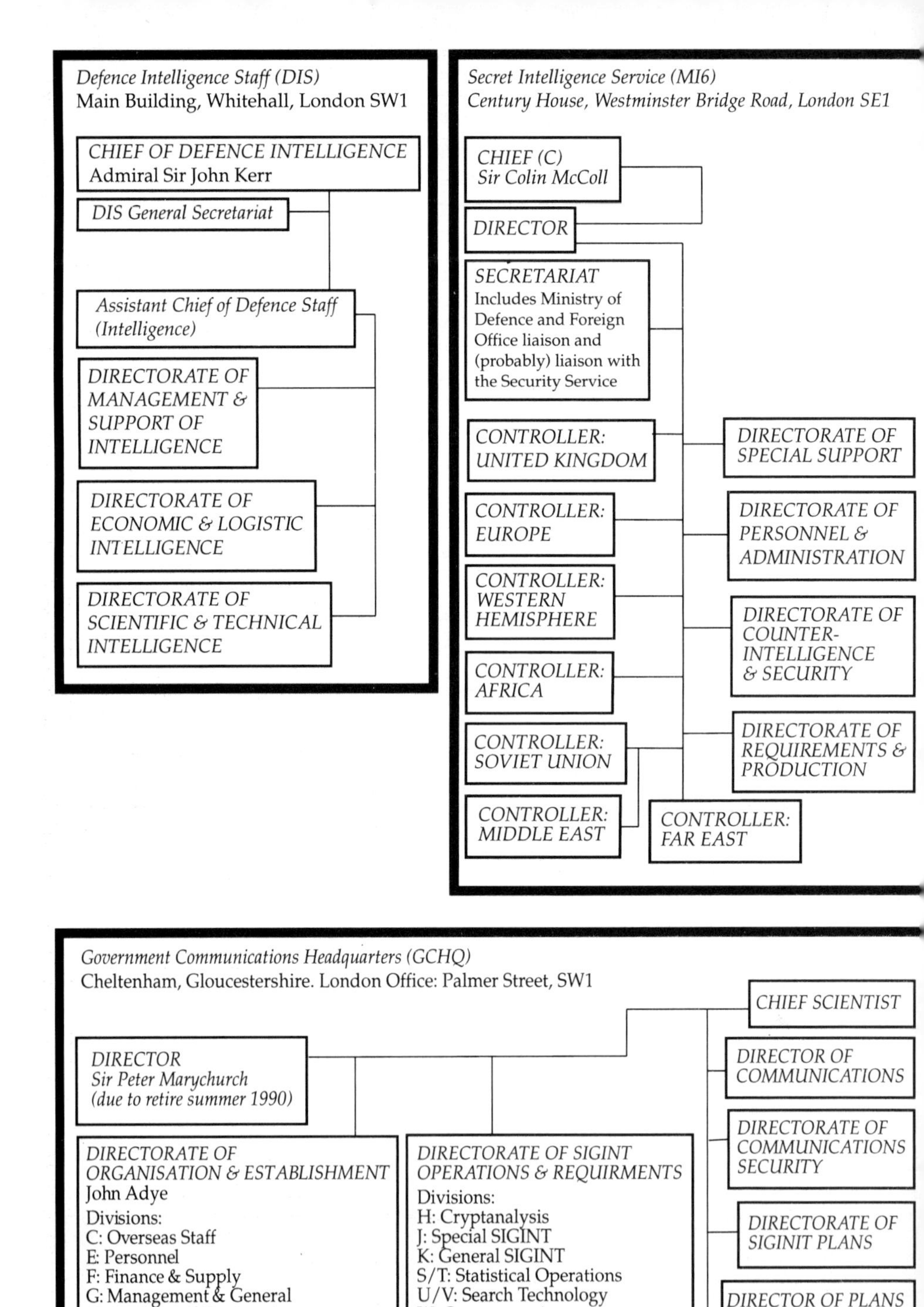

Defence Intelligence Staff (DIS)
Main Building, Whitehall, London SW1
CHIEF OF DEFENCE INTELLIGENCE
Admiral Sir John Kerr
DIS General Secretariat
Assistant Chief of Defence Staff (Intelligence)
DIRECTORATE OF MANAGEMENT & SUPPORT OF INTELLIGENCE
DIRECTORATE OF ECONOMIC & LOGISTIC INTELLIGENCE
DIRECTORATE OF SCIENTIFIC & TECHNICAL INTELLIGENCE
Secret Intelligence Service (MI6)
Century House, Westminster Bridge Road, London SE1
CHIEF (C)
Sir Colin McColl
DIRECTOR
SECRETARIAT
Includes Ministry of Defence and Foreign Office liaison and (probably) liaison with the Security Service
CONTROLLER: UNITED KINGDOM
CONTROLLER: EUROPE
CONTROLLER: WESTERN HEMISPHERE
CONTROLLER: AFRICA
CONTROLLER: SOVIET UNION
CONTROLLER: MIDDLE EAST
CONTROLLER: FAR EAST
DIRECTORATE OF SPECIAL SUPPORT
DIRECTORATE OF PERSONNEL & ADMINISTRATION
DIRECTORATE OF COUNTER-INTELLIGENCE & SECURITY
DIRECTORATE OF REQUIREMENTS & PRODUCTION
Government Communications Headquarters (GCHQ)
Cheltenham, Gloucestershire. London Office: Palmer Street, SW1
DIRECTOR
Sir Peter Marychurch
(due to retire summer 1990)
CHIEF SCIENTIST
DIRECTOR OF COMMUNICATIONS
DIRECTORATE OF COMMUNICATIONS SECURITY
DIRECTORATE OF SIGINIT PLANS
DIRECTOR OF PLANS & POLICY STAFF
DIRECTORATE OF ORGANISATION & ESTABLISHMENT
John Adye
Divisions:
C: Overseas Staff
E: Personnel
F: Finance & Supply
G: Management & General
M: Mechanical Engineering
Q: Technical
R: Security
DIRECTORATE OF SIGINT OPERATIONS & REQUIRMENTS
Divisions:
H: Cryptanalysis
J: Special SIGINT
K: General SIGINT
S/T: Statistical Operations
U/V: Search Technology
W: Communcations
X: Computer Services
Z: Liaison

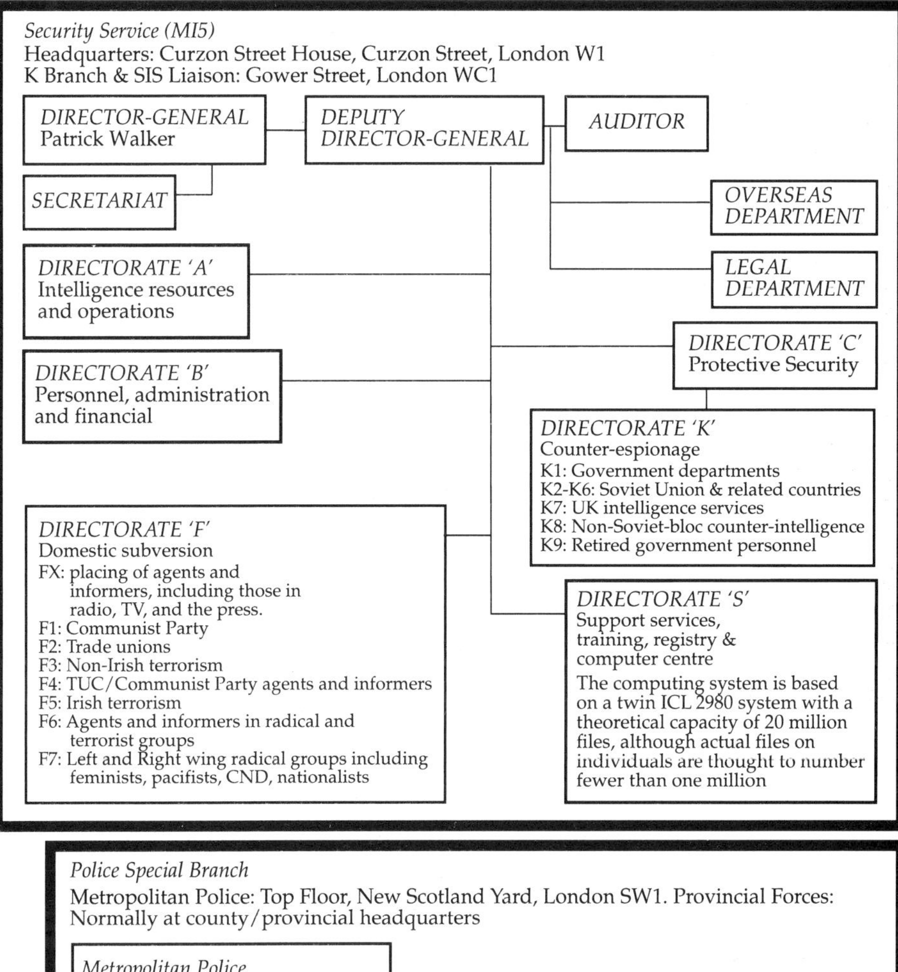


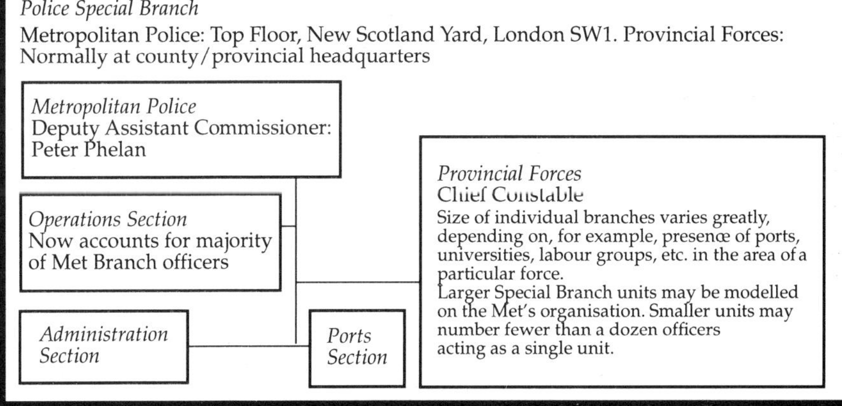


*Security-related units*

A variety of units attached to government departments, the armed forces and even privatised industries have security functions. The more significant of these are:

- Ministry of Defence Police
- UK Atomic Energy Authority Constabulary
- Post Office
- British Telecom
- Special Air Service
- Special Boat Squadron

## The SAS

The Special Air Service (SAS) is classed as a regiment under the Ministry of Defence, with two of its four squadrons assigned to NATO. But it is now firmly established as a highly-trained, armed unit permanently available to the security services and the prime minister.

The SAS has become the armed military wing of the security and intelligence services. In Malaysia in the 1950s and more recently in Northern Ireland, the SAS has become an established anti-terrorist force. But its role in other incidents – being asked to deal with prison riots, for example – blurs the distinction between military and civilian operations and raises so far unanswered questions about its relationship with the police and civil authorities.

On May 19, 1988 – shortly after four SAS men shot dead three unarmed IRA terrorists in Gibraltar – Margaret Thatcher told the Commons: 'We do not discuss matters relating to the SAS, and no one would want to do so unless he wished to undermine the security of this country.'[2]

The Gibraltar operation was controlled by MI5, though the SAS would not have acted without the personal authority of Thatcher. By convention – not by law or as a consequence of Parliament's democratic control – no British military personnel can engage in aggressive action without the say-so of the prime minister. Special portable satellite dishes give SAS units a unique ability to be in permanent touch with Whitehall, either directly or via their Hereford base, wherever they are in the world. Gibraltar, as a colony, was an easy place for the SAS to strike.

## The Immigration Suspect Index

Officials in the Home Office Immigration Service report to MI5 the movements of individuals on a secret Suspect Index. The Index is kept at ports of entry. It lists about 200 names, classified according to different security codes which alert why and with what degree of urgency information about their movements should be passed on to MI5:

- 'J' is the highest security code, signalling immigration officers to communicate directly with MI5 as a matter of urgency and without raising the suspicions of the individual in question.

- 'A' means that MI5 should be informed of the individual's movements as a matter of routine, rather than urgency.

This list has included the actress Vanessa Redgrave, former student activist Tariq Ali, Professor Victor Allen of Leeds University and informal adviser to Arthur

Scargill, and Gerry Lawless, former chair of the Labour group on Hackney Council. Their names were placed in the same category as suspected members of the IRA and suspected terrorists, right-wing extremists and Sikh militants. Other codes with lower priority include: 'O' (refer to Customs); 'V' (violent); 'P' (refer to Special Branch).

In 1988 *The Observer* newspaper obtained a copy of the Suspect Index.[3] It disclosed that Edward Best, a respected British scholar specialising in Central America, was classed as a 'J' subject. This placed him in the company of a suspected Soviet agent and an arms dealer accused of having sold military equipment to Libya. Edward Best received this classification because he is married to a Salvadorean citizen. His wife was a member of a musical group whose songs, according to *The Observer*, were critical of a former El Salvador leader in the early 1970s. Best's work was described as balanced and perceptive by Dr Robert O'Neill, Chichele Professor of History of War at Oxford University and a former director of the International Institute for Strategic Studies, where Best used to study.[4]

## Computer links

There is a long-standing convention that personal information kept by one Whitehall department – the Department of Social Security, for example – for a particular purpose will not be passed to another – the Home Office, for instance. This convention is consistently broken.[5]

Peter Wright described in *Spycatcher* how in the 1970s MI5 established a direct link to the National Insurance (NI) computer in Newcastle, thereby giving it access to files on more than 50 million people. 'In the past', he wrote, 'of course we had always been able to get material from the NI records if we really wanted it. We had a couple of officers posted up there undercover. But establishing a direct computer link was something completely different.'[6]

Local Department of Employment offices have helped the police and Driver and Vehicle Licensing Centre (DVLC) at Swansea track down the addresses of benefit claimants, and vice versa. This is a run-of-the-mill exchange of information. Once individuals are readily identified by one single NI number and the new Government Data Network linking such departments as the Inland Revenue, the Department of Employment, the Department of Social Security, Customs and Excise and the Home Office, is fully operational, it will be much easier for thousands of civil servants as well as MI5 to build up files of personal information to which they will have immediate access.[7] Eric Howe, the Government's Data Protection Registrar, has repeatedly tried – and at the time of writing, is still failing – to get Whitehall permanent secretaries to give him the terms of the voluntary guidelines covering the transfer of information between government departments. But even if he does succeed he is unlikely to be told how MI5 can get access to personal information. And under the terms of the Data Protection Act individual citizens in Britain have no way of knowing what information is kept on them by the security services and how accurate it is. This information can be withheld on the grounds of 'national security'.

Two respected authors have noted that:

> Orwell's fictional design for the year 1984 was not completed on time or to its original specification. But many key elements of technocratic autocracy are available today. Government departments and agencies now hold one and half *billion* personal computer records. By the year 2000, public sector databanks will probably store more than 600 gigabytes (about one hundred thousand million words) of personal information, accessible from one hundred thousand computer terminals; no one will be excluded. Every day, a new government office is computerised. Central government will remain the largest holder and processor of personal information for the foreseeable future, followed closely by other public agencies such as the police service.[8]

## *Police intelligence*

Together MI5 and the Special Branch hold about three million personal records on computer. MI5 has a secret national network of an estimated 200 access terminals and many smaller computers linked to its headquarters in Curzon Street. Since 1966 all police forces have been asked to appoint local intelligence officers, usually inside major police stations. Their task is to assemble a 'memory databank' on anyone who 'comes to the notice' of the police with the help of informants.[9] But the country's largest and at the same time most frequently used electronic database is the Police National Computer (PNC), based in Hendon, north-west London. It stores about 34 million records on a vehicle-owners' register and five million files on a criminal names register.

These indices are not simply lists of basic factual information. The police can enter comments alongside the names, addresses, and the date of birth encoded on driving licences of vehicle-owners or individuals on the criminal names register.

For example, in 1977 a police patrol checked a car parked in a service area on the M6 motorway. The PNC record stated that the owner was 'a prominent member of the Anti-Blood Sports League'. Later that year, the Home Office acknowledged that 'information about association with an organisation' was kept on the PNC.[10]

The Lindop Committee (set up to consider data protection legislation before the Data Protection Act came into force) found, in another example, that one car record included a note that the vehicle was believed to have been used in a bank robbery. Noting that the Home Office had acknowledged that the criminal record index was 'not entirely accurate or complete', the Committee commented that 'the linking of factual personal information about an identifiable individual with speculative data about criminal activity could pose a grave threat to that individual's interests.'[11]

The PNC – the largest police intelligence system in Europe – can be accessed from about 800 terminals installed in police stations around the country. According to a 1986 Home Office circular, those with official authority to apply to the police for information from the PNC include all government departments, postmasters, banks, survey and research bodies, magistrates, hospitals, local authorities, the UK Atomic Energy Authority and solicitors acting in divorce cases. About 120,000 calls are made to the PNC every day. In February 1989, the Home Office minister, Douglas Hogg, claimed that information from the PNC was disclosed only in 'tightly-drawn circumstances'. He was speaking after three police officers and five private detectives were given suspended prison sentences at Winchester Crown Court for misusing PNC files, at times simply for money. Gary Murray, a former private detective whose evidence led to the Winchester convictions, said this was just the tip of the iceberg. He claimed that information on PNC files had regularly been given to private investigators and vetting agencies.[12]

The PNC may be an efficient way to store information and help in the speedy identification of offenders. But experience with the PNC has shown that whatever formal rules are laid down covering access to the information and the way it is to be used, there will be abuses.

Moreover, by a process of accretion, more and more information on individuals is being collected centrally by the police. Scotland Yard has an anti-terrorist squad; there is a National Drugs Intelligence Unit, a national unit to monitor acid house parties and a National Football Intelligence Unit. In the run-up to 1992 and the likelihood of increased co-operation between European police forces, both David Waddington, the Home Secretary, and Sir Peter Imbert, the Metropolitan Police Commissioner, have proposed the creation of a national detective agency, a kind of British FBI.[13]

## Freelancers and 'sleepers'

The police have traditionally used informers in the fight against crime. The security forces and intelligence agencies have used informers and 'supergrasses' in Northern Ireland. MI6 and MI5 use freelance agents, or 'sleepers', for one-off jobs, and particularly for 'deniable' operations – that is to say, where they can deny their involvement if things go wrong. Freelance agents – businessmen, for example – also have the advantage of providing a convenient cover.

- MI5 used Stephen Ward to try and lure the assistant Soviet naval attaché, Yevgeny Ivanov, into a 'honeytrap' during the Profumo affair of the early 1960s. But when the affair ran out of control, Henry Brooke, the Home Secretary, encouraged the police to charge Ward with a convenient offence. Ward was charged with living off immoral earnings. At his trial, MI5 disowned him. Lord Denning's report on the affair made no reference to the role of MI5. Twenty-five years later, the MI5 officer who approached Ward and used the case-name Woods told the authors of a study of the affair that Ward's version of events at his trial – including his account of how he was approached by the Security Service – was correct. Asked if MI5 could not have found a way to have confirmed that Ward was working for the Security Service, the officer replied: 'Yes. Ward might have been alive today had that happened.'[14]

- In 1973, Kenneth and Keith Littlejohn were given long prison sentences for a Dublin bank robbery. They said at their trial that they were put up to it by British intelligence as part of an attempt to discredit the IRA. Kenneth alleged that he had been approached by the then junior Defence Minister, Geoffrey Johnson-Smith. Wanted for an English bank raid, he claimed he was promised immunity from prosecution. They infiltrated the Republican movement and claimed to have bombed two police stations and had been given a gun by MI6. At the Dublin trial they were disowned by MI6 though the Government opened extradition hearings, insisting for 'national security' reasons that they had to be held in secret. During the ensuing parliamentary row, the Home Secretary, Robert Carr, admitted that Kenneth Littlejohn had been working with MI6 and had been in touch with a Special Branch chief inspector. But the Government continued to deny that it had approved any illegal activities and calls for an inquiry were rejected because of 'a long-established rule that we do not discuss the activities of the intelligence services in public'.[15]

- Anthony Divall was what MI6 calls an 'approved unofficial agent'. He provided the initial intelligence which led to the capture of the ship, *Claudia*, off the Irish coast in 1973 when it was seized with Joe Cahill, a former chief of staff of the provisional IRA, and five tonnes of Libyan arms on board. At the height of the Falklands conflict in May 1982 he fooled an Argentine arms-buying mission in Europe. He was asked by MI6 to penetrate the mission based in Paris, and posing as an arms dealer, discover its shopping list. Divall had to show he had the resources, so MI6 arranged for £16 millions to be made available through the Whitehall branch of

Williams & Glyn's bank. The operation effectively sucked in the Argentine arms buyers, giving them the impression they were on to a good deal.

- In 1979, Bill Graham, a former prison officer, military policeman, and Ministry of Defence security official, was approached by a friend in the Special Branch after he had set up a small building company. He was then put in touch with an MI6 officer and asked to apply for a contract to double-glaze the Soviet Trade Mission in Highgate, north London. Graham said he bugged the mission, collected documents and secretly took photographs inside the mission for over two years. He described the operation – which led to the expulsion of three Soviet officials – in a book, *Break-In,* published in June 1987.[16] This was just at the time the Government was trying to ban *Spycatcher* which described operations well before those in the Graham book. But Graham's publisher, Bodley Head, said that it had no problems with the Government. Indeed the Government had given the impression that it wanted to encourage the book.

- David Coghlan, a former army electronics technician, told Yorkshire Television in its 'First Tuesday' programme in April 1988 that he bugged a Militant Tendency office in Liverpool in 1982 on behalf of MI5.[17]

The use of freelancers by the security services continues to this day.

## The revolving door into private security companies

There has been a long-standing practice whereby government officials leave the public service and take their expertise to the private sector. In particular, retired senior armed forces officers have taken on jobs with large defence contractors such as Marconi. Former officials have been attracted by the offer of high salaries to those companies who can use their knowledge of, and contacts in, Whitehall. In one notable example, Sir Brian Tovey, a former director of GCHQ, moved to a top job in 1983 with Plessey, the electronic communications and defence equipment firm, before he resigned and left his GCHQ post (just before the announcement of the union ban at GCHQ in January 1984). Plessey is one of GCHQ's main suppliers and has won contracts for British Telecom's new system X as well as Whitehall's own computer data network.

But much less noticed is the growth of private security companies which employ or have been set up by former intelligence and special forces officers and recruit their former colleagues. They have been encouraged by a combination of different factors: the growth of industrial espionage, the perceived threat of international terrorism and a simple commercial appreciation that there is an expanding market.

In law these firms have no more powers than the ordinary citizen. Nor do private detective agencies – unlike in the US, they do not even have to be licensed. *The Observer* reported in August 1988 how a former senior police officer – Brian McNeil, who had been a detective chief inspector in the Metropolitan Police – agreed to monitor a bugged telephone. According to a spokesman for the Institute of Private Investigators: 'There are quite literally no checks on private detectives. Men can come out of prison and become one. We have no idea how many there are – tens of thousands probably.'[18]

According to his *Handbook of Security*, Peter Hamilton is a former army intelligence officer who had a period of what he calls 'secondment to the Security Service (MI5)'.[19] He has run Zeus Security which the *Daily Star* reported in June 1985 had been set up to 'investigate the fidelity and character of persons, firms or companies and make confidential reports thereon to customers and others'. It has described its tasks as 'to provide security services of all kinds to government and other authorities'. In 1983, Hamilton was employed to monitor objectors at the public inquiry into the Sizewell B nuclear reactor. Hamilton passed the work – sub-contracting is routine in the private security business – to a Norwich firm, Sapphire Investigations Bureau, which in turn contracted a private investigator, Victor Norris, a convicted child abuser and former member of the National Front. He was told in a briefing sheet: 'Client wishes to ascertain identities of principal objectors' at the Sizewell inquiry. 'If possible', it added, 'obtain list of objectors, their connections with media, political leaning, etc.'

David Coghlan, another freelance investigator, claims to have supplied bugging equipment to Hamilton. Coghlan claims he was called in to bug anti-nuclear protest meetings. 'What you have got to realise', he said, 'is that we were told that these people were sinister subversives who were controlled from behind the Iron Curtain and not legitimate protesters who were worried about the building of a power station.'[20]

Hamilton's companies are a good example of how the private security industry can attract a network of former intelligence officers, police officers, businessmen and even politicians. In 1981 Lord Chalfont, the former Labour minister and deputy chairman of the Independent Broadcasting Authority, joined the Zeus board. Chalfont served in Malaysia and Cyprus with Hamilton. He became a consultant to Hamilton's two existing companies, Peter Hamilton (Security Consultants) and Securipol. Those whom Hamilton attracted to the Zeus board included Major General Sir Philip Ward, former commanding officer of the army's London district, and Sir James Starritt, a former head of Scotland Yard's Special Branch.

A number of private security companies have also developed international connections. Jeremy Wetherell was one of the MI5 officers in the special K5 group set up to monitor Wilson and his associates. According to Hamilton's *Handbook of Security*, he worked 'in four continents for government departments and companies on security matters, before becoming manageing director of Lynx Security Services Ltd.

Control Risks, set up in 1973 by a group of former intelligence and special forces officers to advise on kidnap insurance and ransom payments, now concentrates on security information through regular reports on international events. The company's advisers and board of directors have included Dr Richard Clutterbuck, former head of the Royal College of Defence Studies; Arish Turle, a former SAS officer, two former chiefs of military intelligence in Northern Ireland – Roger Meares and Peter Goss; Sir Robert Mark, former Metropolitan Police Commissioner; and Sir Clive Rose, former head of the Civil Contingencies Unit in the Cabinet Office.

Private security companies, mainly based in London, are proliferating. Some – for example, Defence Systems Ltd, set up by Alistair Morrison, the SAS major who advised the West German commando raid during the hijack of a Lufthansa aircraft at Mogadishu in 1977 – concentrate on providing conventional security advice. Others have dealt in murkier waters. In 1977, after the capture of British mercenaries in Angola, the Government introduced legislation making it illegal to recruit mercenaries in Britain. Yet, through an unofficial 'circuit', London remains a centre for mercenary recruitment.

## Employment vetting links

MI5 and the Special Branch also have links with the security and personnel departments of private companies, such as defence contractors, and privatised utilities, like British Telecom. As we have seen, a security officer of a company seeking details on members of his workforce is more likely to approach the local Special Branch than MI5. The SB would, however, contact MI5 if it wanted more information. On occasion MI5 passes information directly to companies about certain of their employees and asks to put its own agents in a firm. In return, MI5 would expect the company's security or personnel section to inform its officers about 'subversive' or troublesome employees. MI5 planted their own agents inside the British Leyland plant at Cowley, Oxford, in the 1970s and early 1980s, a time when a number of militant left-wingers were shop stewards. Secret vetting of employees was revealed in 1983 when 13 BL workers were sacked for supplying false references. They were all members of the International Marxist Group.[21]

## *The Economic League*

MI5 and police Special Branches also have an unofficial, informal relationship with private employment-vetting agencies. Chief among them is the Economic League which has secret files containing, according to the League's own estimate, the names of 30,000 people. In 1986 alone over 200,000 people were checked through its system by subscribing companies. Information is culled from informers and newspaper articles. The information records the organisations, such as the Anti-Apartheid Movement, to which the individuals on its files belong. Much of it is inaccurate, based on hearsay. Its files are protected from the Data Protection Act because they are kept on paper rather than on computer. It does not allow outsiders, including people who suspect it stores information on them, to have access to the files.[22]

Today, the League describes one of its aims as combating 'subversion' in industry and commerce. To this end it keeps files on left-wingers, Labour MPs, trade unions and members of pressure groups – information and allegations which, in its view, may be of interest to its 2,000 or so subscribing member companies. The League also has informal links with the police. In an interview for Granada Television's 'World in Action' programme in February 1988, Michael Noar, the League's Director-General, said:

> As far as the police is concerned, of course the police and Special Branch are interested in some of the things that we are interested in. They follow the activities of these groups in much the same way as we do and therefore they do get in touch with us from time to time and talk to us and say, 'were you at this demonstration or that?' Obviously we help them where we can. If we come across things that we think will be of particular interest to them we send it to them. Now obviously, again in the course of discussions, there is an exchange of information, just in the ordinary course of talking.[23]

Home Office guidelines for the Special Branch specifically forbid the disclosure of information to industrial organisations. The Economic League also has informal links with private security companies. Peter Hamilton, a veteran security consultant, told Gary Murray, a former private investigator, in August 1985: 'Yes, well, I know them (the League) very well of course because I do jobs for them from time to time.' Noar, when questioned, did not deny the League had used Hamilton and recommended its member companies to employ him.

Richard Brett, former regional director of the League's north-west region and a retired army officer with experience in military intelligence, said in December 1988: 'I feel that the League, as presently constituted, is a danger to the democratic way of life in this country. You have got the control of the job prospects of some thousands of people in the hands of one man. It is a situation unparalleled in this country in peacetime.'[24]

John Alderson, the former Devon and Cornwall Chief Constable, told 'World in Action' on February 1, 1988: 'I would regard the Economic League – which is an organisation unaccountable, unofficial, funded by business management – prying into legitimate political activity as absolutely outrageous ... I think the whole business of unofficial organisations taking this on themselves is highly dangerous. We've seen this in Europe before – unofficial organisations becoming a police force which is unaccountable. It's highly dangerous and quite improper.'[25]

## Links with research groups

The intelligence services have also had connections with some right-wing institutions or research organisations, which in turn have links with the media.

### *Forum World Features*

Up until 1966 a CIA front, the Paris-based Congress for Cultural Freedom, secretly funded the London news agency, Forum World Features. Two years later, in response to a request for information from Richard Helms, the then CIA director, Cord Meyer, the CIA's station chief in Britain, stated that the agency was 'run with the knowledge of British Intelligence.' The agency attracted innocent journalists and successfully placed its stories in newspapers throughout the world.

A former *Economist* journalist, Brian Crozier, headed Forum between 1965 and 1975. In 1970 Crozier also set up the Institute for the Study of Conflict. The Institute soon became part of a network with links to intelligence agencies and the right wing of the Conservative Party. Crozier brought in some like-minded colleagues, including Robert Moss, who later helped to set up the National Association for Freedom and became a speech writer for Margaret Thatcher, drafting the first 'Iron Lady' speech.

### *The Institute for the Study of Conflict*

The Institute was set up with the help of funds from two publishing magnates, John Hay Whitney and Richard Mellon Scaife. Both men were at one time closely connected with intelligence agency covert action. It is alleged that Whitney's charitable trust received $325,000 from a CIA conduit fund in 1964.[26] Scaife, recently involved with the US Heritage Fund (enthusiastically backed by President Reagan and Margaret Thatcher) was a partner with the American publisher John McGoff, who was used by the South African Department of Information to acquire media influence in the US in the late 1970s.

'It is no secret', says a former researcher at the Institute, 'that many of [Crozier's] visitors were from the intelligence community'. Other visitors included leading Conservative politicians. 'Crozier', the former researcher adds, 'became preoccupied with post-disaster planning: a blueprint for political renewal after social collapse. He believed that the era of party democracy was nearing its close and that after a period of authoritarian rule political parties should be abolished and power vested in an oligarchical elite from among whom voters would choose their representative.'[27]
Crozier's contacts included:

- Former senior MI6 officer, Nicholas Elliott.
- General Sir Walter Walker, who set up the group, Civil Assistance.
- Founder of the SAS, Colonel David Sterling.
- Airey Neave MP, a close associate of Mrs Thatcher. He was her chief political adviser and Conservative spokesman on Northern Ireland before he was killed by a bomb planted by the Irish National Liberation Army in 1979.
- Conservative Central Office official, Peter Shipley. He later worked in Mrs Thatcher's policy unit at 10 Downing Street.
- Former intelligence co-ordinator at the Cabinet Office, Sir John Tomkinson.

## *The Information Research Department*

One of the Institute's principal British connections was the Information Research Department (IRD), a shady Foreign Office agency closely allied to MI6 and funded by the Secret Vote. It was set up in 1947 by Christopher Mayhew, a junior Labour FO minister (now a Liberal Democrat peer) and, ironically, one of its first officials was Guy Burgess. Its task was to spread anti-Communist propaganda by distributing background articles to favoured British and foreign journalists and commissioning books under the imprint of Ampersand. Michael Goodwin, who succeeded Crozier as director of the Institute, was an editor of Ampersand's Bellman Books series. Among its publications was a loose-leaf manual, *The IRA – Aims, Policy, Tactics*, which it delivered to groups and individuals, including the Institute for the Study of Conflict. IRD was closed down by Dr David Owen, Foreign Secretary, in 1977. The last head of IRD was Ray Whitney, now Conservative MP for Wycombe.

## European and international links

As we have seen, Britain and its closest allies regularly exchange information, especially the results of satellite reconnaissance and signals intelligence (SIGINT) acquired through eavesdropping. US intelligence stations in Britain are in the long run more important than its nuclear bomber bases. The close ties that bind the US and the UK have survived such embarrassing scandals as those involving Philby, Burgess, Maclean and – latterly – Geoffrey Prime.

MI6, MI5 and GCHQ have liaison officers in Washington, and the CIA and the Federal Bureau of Investigation (FBI), have a liaison group in London. More recently, Whitehall has been drawn into closer and regular co-operation with other EC countries. The Trevi Group – EC interior ministers (for Britain, the Home Secretary) – regularly meets to discuss terrorism, drug-smuggling and a common approach to general security issues in the run-up to 1992 and the plan to abandon internal EC frontier controls.

The security services of EC member states now share a hot-line and a network of coded facsimile (fax) machines. The new climate and machinery of co-operation worked well during the surveillance of the IRA team planning an attack in Gibraltar in March 1988, though the controversy over the killing of the three IRA terrorists has led to recriminations between the British and Spanish security forces (see Chapter Six). Also, misunderstandings between the British and Belgian security authorities led to the premature arrest of the suspected Irish terrorist, Father Patrick Ryan, in Brussels in June 1988.

It is clear Margaret Thatcher does not have great trust in Britain's EC partners. She made scathing attacks against the Belgian and Irish governments during the Ryan affair and she does not hide her instinctive belief that Britain's EC partners are soft on terrorism. And in spite of the closer co-operation between EC security forces on a practical level, the Government is extremely wary of plans for institutionalised co-operation.

There has also been friction between British and West German security and intelligence agencies. Whitehall accused the West Germans of a lack of co-operation during the 1989 investigation into the Lockerbie Pan Am airliner disaster. Britain, meanwhile, did not inform West German intelligence about plans to recruit agents to get information about IRA activity against the British Army on the Rhine (BAOR).[28]

When it comes to intelligence gathering, governments are out for what they can get; there is no room for moral considerations. For example, there have been occasions when the decision to allow refugees into Britain or not has depended on whether they have agreed to provide information about political developments in the country from which they were fleeing. Such is the appetite for 'intelligence' that intelligence agencies will resort to any means to get it.[29]

# CHAPTER SIX

# Security and Intelligence Operations

It will take a long time before reform and revolution will convince the security and intelligence services to reconsider their traditional targets – Eastern Europe and the Soviet Union. There is not only the deeply-held prejudice, entrenched in bodies like the security services, that 'once a Communist, always a Communist', but the view that uncertainty increases rather than diminishes the need to monitor the activities of those countries. And despite the obvious priority target – violent terrorism – the British security and intelligence bureaucracy is pursuing easy targets with increasing vigour: undermining foreign, and often friendly, governments by intercepting their communications, eavesdropping on the communications of foreign companies and private banks, and targeting domestic groups and private individuals considered 'subversive' or 'potentially subversive'.

In pursuit of their targets the security and intelligence services continue to use defectors and informers – notoriously unreliable – and the weapons of disinformation and official leaks. They also use other weapons famous throughout the world – hidden microphones, telephone-taps (with the help of British Telecom), infiltrators, informers, burglary, mail-opening (in co-operation with the Post Office), watching and following. And with increasing enthusiasm, they are adopting new methods, including probe microphones and bugs which do not require physical entry into property.

## Telephone-tapping

The practice of telephone-tapping, both authorised and unauthorised, is increasing steadily – partly because the security and intelligence services perceive an increasing threat, and partly because it is becoming so much easier to intercept telephone communications and store the contents of the conversations.

An investigation by *The Observer* newspaper in October 1988 estimated that 30,000 individual lines were tapped each year at an annual cost of about £10 million and that the number of British Telecom (BT) tapping engineers – 80 – had increased by 50 percent over the decade.[1] The latest known tapping centre is at BT's former headquarters building in Gresham Street in the City of London. It has more than 1,000 lines, but switching mechanisms mean that it can deal with many more thousands of incoming intercepted calls.

However, this does not take into account the enormous capacity for interception by GCHQ computers and eavesdropping stations. Figuratively speaking, GCHQ – which has taken over many of the tapping operations from

MI5 – 'harvests' the air-waves. The potentially enormous burden of transcribing all the communications that are intercepted is allayed by increasingly sophisticated computers that can scan tapes for trigger words, names and particular telephone numbers.

Another reason why it is impossible to know how many wires have been tapped is the traditional Home Office practice of issuing a single warrant for the entire membership, or suspected membership, of targeted groups and organisations rather than issuing an individual warrant for each individual tap. There have been questions, too, about whether MI5 always bothers to get a warrant before it applies a tap. Certainly, Peter Wright records in *Spycatcher* how he sometimes placed taps without going through official procedures. *Police Review* in February 1985 quoted a source inside British Telecom as saying that 'the security services never produce warrants when making phone taps'. The source added: 'The normal procedure, we were told, is for a specially employed squad of telephone engineers to visit an exchange at night to make the necessary links. When it is a police matter, we always see the warrant. When the tap is being made for the security services, we never see the warrant. We never know if there is one.'[2]

## The Interception of Communications Act

In 1985 Parliament passed the Interception of Communications Act. In common with the 1989 Security Service Act, this measure was forced upon ministers by the European Convention on Human Rights. In the 1984 Malone case the European Court criticised the Government because of the absence of any legal controls over tapping. As a result, the 1985 Act established a tribunal to investigate complaints and the post of a commissioner – at present, Lord Justice Lloyd – charged with monitoring the extent of tapping and with presenting an annual report to Parliament.

But the tribunal's terms of reference were cleverly and narrowly defined. It can investigate whether a tap was wrongly authorised – that is to say whether the criteria for the issue of a warrant were observed. But it cannot take any action in the event of an illegal tap – one that is made without a warrant. Individuals cannot know whether their phones are tapped or not and therefore whether they are the object of illegal interceptions. They cannot know the reason for the tribunal's decisions and have no right of appeal to a civil court against its conclusions.

In his latest annual report, Lord Justice Lloyd said that on December 31, 1988 there were 225 tapping warrants issued by the Home Secretary in force, and 27 by the Scottish Secretary. These statistics applied only to that day – in the course of 1988 the Home Secretary had authorised a total of 412 warrants. But the figures do not present a full picture. The number of warrants issued by the Foreign Secretary and the Northern Ireland Secretary, for example, are not published. And as we have seen, one warrant can cover an entire organisation. As Lloyd put it: 'One warrant, though it must contain only one target, may contain more than one line. This is because the "one particular person" who must be specified or described in the warrant may be one particular organisation or one particular association or combination of persons. Obviously an organisation may have more than one line.' He also noted that the monitoring of conversations of other people who happen to use the same line as that deemed likely to be used by the target named in the warrant is justified by the Interception of Communications Act.[3]

In his first report, for the year 1986, Lloyd suggested that the Special Branch should end its then practice of applying for a one-month renewal for warrants and instead apply for the six-month extension allowed under the Act. Requiring renewals too frequently might not only overburden the Home Secretary but could jeopardise detecting threats to national security, he said.

> Weeks or months may go by with little or nothing of value being obtained. Yet it is that interception which may in the end produce (and has in my experience in fact produced) the vital piece of intelligence which enables the police to mount, for example, a successful operation in the field of counter terrorism.[4]

Most – an estimated three out of four – taps are made for reasons judged to relate to 'national security' rather than to target criminals.[5] Some, such as those directed at certain embassies, are more or less permanent.[6] Lloyd's annual reports are submitted to the Prime Minister who can censor them – there is no way of knowing – before they are presented to Parliament. Lloyd could complain and ultimately resign, if he believes the Government is covering up malpractice. But even if he were to do so, the new Official Secrets Act, which imposes a blanket ban on the disclosure of information about telephone-tapping, would prevent him from speaking out.

The Interception of Communications Act also covers mail delivered through the post. But it does not cover modern bugging devices. Nor does it cover the new computer-run telephone exchange system, System X. This system, developed by Plessey – which has close links with GCHQ – uses digital signals which enables BT and the security and intelligence services to trace and store telephone calls much more easily. The tapper no longer has to tamper physically with individual lines, telephone exchanges or office switchboards. Lines can be tapped by remote interception. Mark Leopold (a former BT employee) and Patrick FitzGerald describe in their book, *Stranger on the Line: The Secret History of Phone Tapping*, how the system escapes the Act: 'the [digital] tap leaves no physical presence anywhere; it is literally invisible and makes no discernible changes to the telephone circuit being tapped.'[7]

The Act states that a minister must guarantee that in the course of an authorised investigation, material which is intercepted but is not covered by a warrant 'is not read, looked at or listened to by any person.' Yet only the examination of *all* the intercepts could show whether the contents conform to the requirements of a minister's certificate for a tap.

## *Obtaining a warrant*

In an affidavit to the Court of Appeal used in the Campaign for Nuclear Disarmament's (CND) failed attempt for a ruling against tapping and surveillance by MI5, Cathy Massiter, the former MI5 officer who made the tapping disclosures, described the official procedure for obtaining a warrant. An MI5 application to the Home Office would be accompanied by a one-paragraph summary of two to three sentences, known as the 'short reason'. This is all the permanent secretary at the Home Office or the home secretary himself would see unless they requested a fuller explanation. The application is initially made by an MI5 desk officer; it then goes to the head of the section, an assistant director, then to the branch director and on to the deputy director-general. The 'short reason' would then be forwarded to the home secretary's office. When the warrant is approved, the deputy director-general would send the file back to the desk officer with a note saying that it had been accepted, though the desk officer would not personally see the warrant.[8]

When Massiter first started to question the propriety of some of the activities she was required to carry out, her superiors suggested she should see a psychiatrist. They then made it clear she should resign; she decided to do so anyway. After leaving MI5 in 1984, she provided a first-hand account of MI5 operations and how they violated their own guidelines in 'MI5's Official Secrets', produced by the independent television company, 20/20 Vision. The programme was initially banned by the Independent Broadcasting Authority (IBA) on the grounds that it would break the Official Secrets Act. But the press and Labour MPs were given a private viewing, and after the IBA lifted its ban, the programme was broadcast on March 8, 1985. The uproar the programme had provoked prior to transmission led the Prime Minister to announce, on February 28, that she had asked Lord Bridge of Harwich, a senior Law Lord and then chairman of the Security Commission, to investigate Massiter's allegations. Lord Bridge reported back within five days (including a weekend) and cleared governments back to 1970 of any improper authorisation of telephone-tapping by MI5. His inquiry covered 2,774 taps which had been authorised between 1980 and 1984 alone. Not surprisingly, his inquiry was greeted with widespread scepticism.

## Monitoring domestic 'subversion'

MI5 and the Special Branch are responsible for countering perceived threats within Britain. After the second world war they concentrated on the Communist bloc, not only its 'official' agents or spies working out of embassies and trade missions, but also those regarded as their allies within the British state, notably the Communist Party of Great Britain. The net widened in the 1960s, and particularly in the early 1970s, when MI5 and the SB enthusiastically went after protest groups, single-issue campaigners and trade union leaders, as well as ideologically extreme organisations on both the left and right. This diversion of attention – and resources – away from K Branch and towards F Branch was resented by some MI5 officers, the so-called 'Young Turks', who were obsessed by alleged Soviet penetration of the Security Service. Peter Wright was among them although it did not stop him from conspiring against Harold Wilson and the Labour leadership in the 1960s and 1970s.

Accumulated evidence suggests that MI5 and the Special Branch simply cannot resist the temptation to collect – and hoard – files on individuals and groups they have confronted, however seriously, however innocently, however indirectly. According to some commentators, anyone belonging to one of the groups below could find themselves on an MI5 or Special Branch file without ever knowing it:

- those who belong to any form of protest group;
- homosexuals and lesbians;
- owners of cars parked near selected political meetings and demonstrations;
- owners of vehicles seen parked near houses owned by suspected or controversial people;
- victims of crimes;
- anyone who makes a complaint to the police;
- anyone who writes controversial letters to the newspapers criticising government policy on sensitive issues such as nuclear policy or who criticises the security services.[9]

More recently MI5 has begun to give priority to helping the Special Branch pursue and investigate violent groups, including the IRA and Middle-East-based terrorists. In response to queries, Whitehall officials say, privately, that only a very small number of MI5 officers now deal with 'domestic subversion' – a task to which GCHQ is increasingly turning its attention. There is no way of substantiating the claims of these officials and both supporters of the Government inside the Commons and its advisers outside have warned that MI5 must not drop its guard against traditional targets despite the upheavals in Eastern Europe, the collapse of Communism's appeal and the decline of the industrial and political muscle of trade unions.

Economic information, meanwhile, is becoming an increasingly important target for Britain's intelligence agencies, notably GCHQ, which has gathered economic intelligence from its early days. Diplomatic messages about international oil negotiations, the investment of oil revenue, national responses to world currency problems and Japan's industrial and economic policies were all priorities for GCHQ in the mid-1970s. Intercepted messages were sent to large British companies, including Rio Tinto-Zinc (RTZ), ICI, and BP.[10] In the 1980s, Sir Peter Middleton, permanent secretary at the Treasury, succeeded in securing a bigger budget for the collection and processing of economic intelligence.[11] Foreign companies and banks themselves are now regarded as legitimate GCHQ targets.

## *The Communist Party of Great Britain (CPGB)*

The CPGB has been a perennial MI5 target; Communist sympathisers along with Fascists were the first targets of the positive vetting system introduced during the Cold War.

In a notorious incident in 1955, code-named 'Party Piece', MI5 officers burgled the Mayfair flat of a wealthy CP member who was responsible for keeping the membership files. One night when the owner of the flat was away, MI5 took all 55,000 files, microfilmed them and returned them before dawn. Twenty years later, builders working at the Party's London headquarters found a microphone hidden in a rostrum. And in the early 1980s, a party official, Betty Reid, unwittingly employed an MI5 agent as her housekeeper.

However, despite the changing international climate and shift in policy and outlook of the CPGB, there remains an obsession with it. It was only relatively recently that MI5 acknowledged that not every contributor to the Party's smart monthly, *Marxism Today*, was a potential 'subversive' or Communist sympathiser. Any Communist link, suspected or known, is, for MI5, a useful benchmark or excuse for targeting, especially at a confusing time of shifting allegiances and extra-parliamentary political activity.

## *The Campaign for Nuclear Disarmament (CND)*

Cathy Massiter disclosed in the 20/20 Vision television programme how the targeting of those engaged in legitimate political dissent led to the surveillance of groups which even MI5 itself did not classify as 'subversive'. She showed how the Government used MI5 for its own party political reasons, flying in the face of the Maxwell-Fyfe Directive. She revealed, too, how the Special Branch broke its guidelines and, in particular, its instruction that 'data on individuals or organisations should not under any circumstances be collected or held solely on the basis that ... a person or organisation supports unpopular causes.'[12]

CND was classed as a 'subversive organisation' by MI5 in the mid-1960s when active members were recorded as Communist sympathisers. By the early 1980s MI5 had dropped this classification. But as CND's popularity rapidly rose, partly because of the controversy over cruise missiles, and as unilateral nuclear disarmament was being adopted as official Labour Party policy, MI5, the SB and the Thatcher Government moved in. Ironically, surveillance of CND was more intense when it was off the official subversive list than when it was on it.

In 1982 MI5 placed an agent called Harry Newton in CND's London headquarters. Newton was a lecturer in trade union studies who knew many of the leading CND officials and provided MI5 with internal CND documents.[13] MI5 instigated this action shortly after refusing a request by Thames Valley Special Branch for money to infiltrate local CND branches on the grounds that it would break MI5's charter.[14]

In March 1983 Stanley Bonnett, the former editor of CND's magazine, *Sanity*, was approached by Special Branch officers. He passed them minutes of CND meetings, lists of over 1,000 activists and information about the politics and private lives of leading CND officers.[15]

That same month Michael Heseltine, then Defence Secretary, set up a special section in his ministry – Defence Secretariat (DS)19 – to counter CND's increasingly popular message. The organisation was headed by John Ledlie, an official who had worked in Northern Ireland and was later appointed chief press officer at the Ministry of Defence. DS19 approached MI5 for information on the political affiliations of leading CND members. Massiter reports that she was told to extract non-classified information about the left-wing associations of CND leaders for use by DS19. Heseltine used the information in speeches during the run-up to the 1983 general election, suggesting that CND was controlled by 'full-time socialists or Communists'. This view was contrary to MI5's own official assessment.

In April 1983 the deputy director-general of MI5 suggested that the telephone of a suitable CND target should be tapped. To avoid any embarrassment, the tap was not placed until after the general election. The target chosen was John Cox, a CND vice-president. Targeting Cox provided MI5 with the advantage of acting against a traditional 'subversive' by virtue of his affiliation to the Communist Party. Their choice had an additional advantage: Cox lived in Wales and used the telephone a good deal to talk to other leading CND officials. The operation provided MI5 with the opportunity to record the attitudes and views of Bruce Kent, CND's general secretary, and Joan Ruddock, CND's chairwoman, now Labour MP for Deptford.

Questioned in 1985, more than a year after he authorised the tap on John Cox, the then Home Secretary, Leon Brittan, told the Commons: 'There is no doubt that lawful campaigning to change the mind of the Government about nuclear disarmament whether unilateral or otherwise is an entirely legitimate activity.'[16]

By then MI5, working with Special Branches throughout the country, had built up files on over 300 members of CND who could not be described as 'subversives' even under its own official definition. According to Cathy Massiter: 'It was a classic example of the way people go on record ... You couldn't just concentrate on the subversive elements of CND, you had to be able to answer questions on the non-subversive elements and the whole thing sort of began to flow into a grey area.'[17]

MI5 had also broken its own internal guidelines on phone-tapping. Although they are not public and do not appear in any statute, they say it is not enough simply to be an active Communist or 'subversive'. The target must be involved in criminal activity liable to three years in gaol or in 'major subversive, terrorist or espionage activity'. The information must relate directly to the 'defence of the realm' and 'normal' methods of investigation must have been tried and failed, or be considered unlikely to succeed. This, Massiter said in her affidavit to the Court of Appeal, was 'manifestly not the case where Cox and CND were concerned'. MI5, according to Massiter, knew from its own work and from other sources within the CP that Cox was *not* 'manipulating CND in a clandestine way', the official grounds on which the warrant had been sought.

Massiter told 20/20 Vision: 'We were violating our own rules. It seemed to be getting out of control. This was happening not because CND, as such, justified this kind of treatment but simply because of political pressure; the heat was there for information about CND and we had to have it.'[18]

In a separate incident, West Midlands Special Branch investigated four anti-nuclear campaigners in Sutton Coldfield after they wrote to their local newspaper in 1981. They protested against the failure of the Government to give Parliament information about nuclear weapons policy. Soon afterwards the women began to be harassed, mainly by telephone calls. A man visited the home of one of them, Madeleine Haigh, saying he was investigating a fraud on a mail-order company. She was told by her local police station that her visitor was not a policeman. After repeatedly unsuccessful attempts to find out what was going on, Haigh approached her MP, the cabinet minister Norman Fowler. She discovered that her visitor was a Special Branch Inspector. He was neither publicly identified, nor disciplined. Sir Philip Knights, the West Midlands Chief Constable, defended the activities of his officers on the grounds that the case 'fell within the terms of reference of the Special Branch.' In a report to his police committee, he said: 'Mrs Haigh had written to a newspaper in terms which were interpreted as indicating that she might be a person prepared to support or get involved in public protests ... the responsibility of Special Branch [is] analysing and assessing information of that kind'.[19]

## *The National Council for Civil Liberties (Liberty)*

*Liberty* (then known as NCCL) was classified as 'subversive' in the mid-1970s. The decision to target the organisation was taken by Charles Elwell, an assistant director in MI5's F Branch. It was justified by the claim that the organisation's criticism of institutions, including the police, amounted to deliberate attempts to undermine them. Massiter said that as a result:

> Anyone who was on the National Executive of the NCCL, who worked for NCCL, or who was an active member to the degree of being, say, a branch secretary of NCCL, would be placed on permanent record. Routine inquiries would be instituted to identify such people ... The police were actually asked to identify branch secretaries in their area and report on the activities of the NCCL.[20]

A Manchester councillor, Tony Mackie, described to 20/20 Vision how a friend made notes for the Special Branch at a *Liberty* meeting addressed by Roy Hattersley, Labour's deputy leader and shadow Home Secretary.

MI5 opened files on Patricia Hewitt, then *Liberty*'s general secretary, and Harriet Harman, then the organisation's legal officer, labelling them 'Communist sympathisers'.

*Liberty* was officially taken off MI5's list of 'subversive organisations' in 1981. However, it could still be a Special Branch target.

## *Trade unions*

The trade union movement and individual union leaders and activists have always been a prime MI5 and Special Branch target. This is particularly the case during periods of industrial action, especially in the public sector and during strikes involving large companies. Unions have been infiltrated, offices bugged and on occasions, private homes burgled. MI5 does not, however, wait for strikes. On May 6, 1968 Barbara Castle noted in her diary: 'One of my discoveries in my new job is that the Minister of Labour has always been furnished with security reports on the trade unions.'[21]

- For over a decade, from 1966 to 1977, MI5 amassed 40 volumes of material on two union leaders, Jack Jones and Hugh (now Lord) Scanlon, who for many years were the twin pillars of the trade union establishment. It sent 'security' reports on their political activities and views to 10 Downing Street, tapped their phones and attempted to block their appointment to top jobs.[22]

- Other trade union activists whose phones have been tapped include Margaret Witham and Mick Duggan of the Civil and Public Services Association. MI5 has also tapped the phone of Ken Gill, a Communist, former chairman of the Trades Union Congress (TUC) and now General Secretary of the white-collar union, Manufacturing, Science and Finance (MSF). In the 1970s MI5 broke into Gill's south London house when his union, Tass, was planning a merger with the engineers.[23]

- Fire Brigade Union officials said on the 20/20 Vision television programme that they believed their phones were tapped during their first-ever strike in 1977. At one negotiating meeting at the Home Office, a union official asked a civil servant: 'Have you buggers been tapping our phone?' The civil servant replied: 'We've got to know what you're gonna do.'[24]

- MI5 has marked down Jack Dromey, a national officer in the Transport and General Workers Union (TGWU) and husband of the Labour MP, Harriet Harman, as 'potentially subversive'. Dromey is a supporter of the Labour leader, Neil Kinnock, and regards himself as a mainstream Labour Party member. Certainly he has little time for the extreme left. MI5 has compiled a permanent file on Dromey. He came to its attention when he was on *Liberty*'s executive committee and when he co-ordinated picketing during the bitter 1977 Grunwick dispute.[25]

- In 1978, the telephone of Syd Harraway, a Communist shop steward convener at Ford's Dagenham plant, was tapped throughout difficult and, for the Government, crucial, pay negotiations. Whitehall wanted to discover the unions' tactics and their private 'bottom line' in negotiations with the company. The information was passed on to the Department of Employment.[26]

- The telephones of miners' leaders – notably Arthur Scargill, the NUM national president, and Mick McGahey, a Communist, former president of the Scottish miners and member of the Scottish TUC – have been tapped. GCHQ advised the Special Branch during the tapping programme directed against striking miners during the 1984-85 dispute.

Cathy Massiter has also confirmed that MI5 has moles inside trade unions who back up information retrieved from phone-tapping. 'Whenever a major dispute came up', she told 20/20 Vision, 'something at Fords or the mines, or the Post Office ... immediately it would become a major area for investigation...'[27] Another former MI5 official said on the same programme that certain telephones were tapped in the late 1970s irrespective of any industrial dispute.

In 1980, in response to a request from a subsection of MI5's counter-subversion desk covering the Communist Party (F1), a Special Branch memorandum was sent to MI5 headquarters in London. Addressed to 'The Director-General, Box 500, Parliament Street', it set out the political and trade union activities of James Hogg, a TGWU shop steward at the Carnation Food factory in Dumfries, Scotland. The document was written by Detective Constable Gordon Hunter of Dumfries CID and signed by Chief Inspector David Kirkwood on behalf of the Chief Constable of Galloway and Dumfries. The report prepared on James Hogg admitted that the alleged connection he had with the Socialist Workers' Party (SWP) was based 'solely on hearsay information ... from inside the factory'. It stated:

> Hogg is a shop steward and a member of the factory negotiating team on behalf of the union at the factory. Hogg has been described by a management contact as being more than usually active in union debates within the factory and is thought of as very left wing. Hogg is thought to be connected with the Socialist Workers' Party also, although this cannot be verified at present ... Hogg cannot proceed any further within the Carnation Food factory either in a work capacity or within the union structure at the factory and it is thought by management that he may well leave sometime in the near future to take up some kind of full-time employment with the TGWU. This situation will obviously be monitored and any further development will be reported ... The text of communication has been noted in respect of Hogg's involvement with the Communist Party of Great Britain and this will of course be watched for any subsequent developments.[28]

Hogg was a quality control inspector. He had no criminal record and was not a member of the SWP or of the Communist Party. He said: 'I am just a shop steward doing my job to try and improve the conditions of my fellow workers.'[29] His security file was numbered 886214.

## *Journalists*

Journalists have been regularly targeted by the security and intelligence services.

- Before the war, MI5 kept a file on Claude Cockburn, editor of *The Week*. In a secret letter to the US embassy Sir Vernon Kell, the first Director-General of MI5, wrote that the paper's articles were 'always written up from the left-wing angle'. He added that there were, however, 'occasions on which Cockburn is quite well informed and by intelligent anticipation gets quite close to the truth.'[30]

- A file discovered by journalist and author Peter Hennessy at the Public Record Office at Kew, escaping the Cabinet Office 'weeders', revealed that MI5 tapped the phone of Paul Einzig, political correspondent of the *Financial Times* between 1945 and 1956 and a leading political journalist. Einzig came to MI5's attention for writing a report in the *Financial Times* in 1946 on 'the Cabinet's reasons for omitting from the white paper on the iron and steel industry any justification of the Government's policy.' MI5 also kept a file on Frederick Kuh, London correspondent of the *Chicago Sun*, who had written a scoop about the 1946 atomic energy bill.[31]

- Anne McHardy of *The Guardian* was one of many British journalists based in Belfast whose phones were tapped under a Labour government in the late 1970s. Transcripts of the recorded tapes were given to Northern Ireland Office information officers.[32]

- In the late 1970s, MI5 official Charles Elwell commissioned a special study on 'subversion in the media'. Its self-appointed task was to monitor what it considered to be anti-establishment views among journalists. It collected information on journalists appointed to what it regarded as politically sensitive and influential, opinion-forming posts. This special exercise was abandoned a few years later but the files remain.[33]

MI5 continues to monitor the activities and sources of individual journalists. Most notably, MI5 has tapped the telephones of Duncan Campbell (whose home was also broken into by Special Branch officers during the Zircon spy satellite controversy in 1987) and Mick Costello, a senior *Morning Star* journalist and former Communist Party official.[34] There is also a branch of the intelligence services which monitors articles written by British journalists about the Government's foreign policy, including their approach towards the EEC.[35]

## *The BBC*

In 1985 BBC management acknowledged for the first time that it vetted all news and current affairs appointments. The exercise was co-ordinated by Brigadier Ronnie Stonham, who was given the title of special assistant to the Director-General. He checked names with MI5. After his role was disclosed by *The Observer*, the BBC said that the vetting system was introduced because of the corporation's official role in war or national emergency. But the vetting net was cast much wider and included, for example, the post of editor of the BBC magazine, *The Listener*. Other enquiries have shown that vetting has extended to makers of drama programmes and the arts.

Following the disclosure, BBC management said that in future vetting would be limited to those staff involved in planning and operating emergency services and those with access to classified information (a broad and unclear criterion, since many current affairs journalists enjoy such access), and those journalists in the external services working in Bush House. It explained that overseas service broadcasters – some of them foreign nationals – could be subject to intimidation while others had access to sensitive information.

Stonham was replaced in 1988 by Michael Hodder, a former Royal Marines officer. Hodder was previously personnel officer for BBC radio news and current affairs, a job which gave him access to personal files. His new title is chief assistant to the BBC's personnel director, Christopher Martin, himself a former Royal Marines officer.

During the Commons debates on the Security Service Bill in January 1989, Merlyn Rees said he was unaware of the MI5/BBC vetting system when he was Home Secretary from 1976 to 1979. He said that in the course of the 1985 controversy over reports that BBC employees were vetted he had written to the Cabinet Secretary, Robert Armstrong, asking if the reports were accurate. He asked Armstrong why he was not told and received a letter back which said: 'You are perfectly right, you were never told.'[36] Yet Rees had been responsible for both broadcasting and MI5.

## *Lawyers and others*

MI5 has opened files on lawyers with radical or left-wing clients. It collected material on Larry Grant, the solicitor who defended the former CIA agent, Philip Agee, who was deported in 1977.[37] Grant also acted for the former MI5 officer, Michael Bettaney, in 1984. MI5 is understood to have tried but failed to get a Home Office warrant to tap the phone of Lord Gifford QC in 1978, on the grounds that he was working with terrorists.[38] Gifford acted for Astrid Proll, the West German wanted in connection with the Baader-Meinhof group.

- In October 1975, Peter Hain, then a leading Young Liberal and chairman of the Stop the Seventy Tour Committee (campaigning against the South African rugby team playing in Britain), was arrested and later tried at the Old Bailey for a bank theft he had not committed. Questions remain about whether he was framed by the South African security service, BOSS, with the help of elements within MI5.

- The Tory MP, Jonathan Aitken, told the Commons in January 1989 that MI5 had listed six Conservative MPs, warning ministers that they should not be appointed to the Government. The suggestion is not that they had any political skeletons in their cupboards or that they were a security risk – rather, that their past personal or financial liaisons could be embarrassing to the Government. Aitken urged MI5 to stop running after what he called 'false scents'.[39]

- During the passage of the new Official Secrets Act through the Commons in January 1989, the senior Tory backbencher, Sir Richard Body, disclosed that when he was an officer in an anti-Common Market organisation in the 1970s – he was already an MP – he received a telephone call and later had a meeting with a member of the security services. He was told that although his good intentions were not doubted, his telephone was being intercepted.[40]

It was during this same debate that Roy Hattersley, the shadow Home Secretary, asked whether if an MI5 officer told him that his telephone had been tapped without a warrant, and therefore illegally, and his home burgled without warrant, and therefore illegally, it would be a criminal offence for him to make that information public? Yes, replied John Patten.[41]

## Northern Ireland

Security and intelligence agencies have fought among themselves for influence and control in Northern Ireland. MI5 has been accused – notably by Captain Fred Holroyd, a former military intelligence officer in Northern Ireland in the 1970s – of indulging in self-defeating 'dirty tricks' with elements of the RUC and promoting a 'shoot to kill' policy in an aggressive attempt to get quick results.[42] MI6, whose presence in the British province has been resented by MI5, has counselled caution and patience, keeping its eye on the need to promote long-term political solutions with the support of the nationalist community and Dublin. The British army, meanwhile, is fighting a guerrilla war of attrition (in co-operation with the civil police), to which its senior officers believe there can be no military solution.

Against this background, there is growing evidence that elements of the security services have indulged in political activities far beyond their task of defeating the Provisional IRA and Loyalist terrorist groups. A former MI5 agent, James Miller, has alleged that the Security Service penetrated the Ulster Defence Association and encouraged the idea of a general strike. The strike in 1974 destroyed the new power-sharing government. Miller later told *The Sunday Times*: 'My case officer told me to do it. MI5 wanted to get at Wilson. They said he was a Soviet agent.'[43]

It has also been suggested that the Social Democratic and Labour Party was set up with the help of the intelligence services. In his book, *Through the Looking Glass* – an account of hidden MI6 influence on foreign policy – the author Anthony Verrier, wrote: 'They – officials, the permanent government – had played a crucial, covert role in the formation of a democratic political party, the Social Democratic and Labour Party, which they saw as an acceptable alternative to the Provisionals.'[44]

Soon after she came to power in 1979, Margaret Thatcher – made aware of the infighting between the different security and intelligence agencies – appointed Sir Maurice Oldfield, the recently retired head of MI6, to a new post of Security Co-ordinator in Northern Ireland. Oldfield, a devout High Church Anglican, concentrated on trying to build up a network of informers and contacts within the Catholic community, including priests. His approach was resented by both sides in the conflict – both Loyalists and the IRA were suspicious of his contacts with the Catholic community. He soon became the victim of a smear campaign. In 1980, he was interviewed by Sir Robert Armstrong, the Cabinet Secretary, and asked about rumours that he was or had been a homosexual. Oldfield admitted that as a student he had indulged in the occasional 'youthful peccadillo' at university more than 40 years earlier and had not mentioned this when he had been vetted.[45] Oldfield, who was regarded as one of the most thoughtful of MI6 chiefs, died of cancer shortly after he left Northern Ireland.

## The Gibraltar Affair

MI5's continuing role in Britain's colonies allowed it to take charge of one of the most controversial, and still unexplained, counter-terrorist operations of recent years: the killing in Gibraltar on March 6, 1988 of three unarmed members of an IRA 'active service unit'. Two years after the incident a number of fundamental questions remain unanswered. If, as the Spanish Government and police maintain, the three terrorists – Danny McCann, Sean Savage and Mairead Farrell – were followed up to the Gibraltar frontier, why were they not arrested? Unnamed Spanish police sources told the respected Madrid newspaper, *El País*, of their 'certainty' that the three were unarmed and had crossed the border without explosives. Why then did MI5 officers tell the SAS soldiers following the IRA team not only that the three were almost certain to be armed, but that they were also likely to have on them a remote-control detonator enabling them to trigger a bomb they had left, primed, down-town? Why if, as was claimed, the Renault car parked by Savage was thought to contain a bomb, was the area around the car not immediately evacuated? Why, since the planned target was the army guard ceremony on the following Tuesday, did MI5 warn the SAS that the IRA team could have been about to detonate a bomb on the Sunday afternoon? One Gibraltar policeman said in evidence to the inquest that those who were following Savage suspected he was fusing a bomb. He added, however, that the suspicion that he had primed a car bomb lasted for no more than a few minutes that Sunday afternoon. A senior MI5 official – called officer O at the coroner's inquest – acknowledged that he made incorrect assumptions about the danger presented by the three IRA members that day, Sunday, March 6.

The suspicion remains that MI5 was determined to deal with the IRA team on British territory rather than leave it to the security authorities in Spain. MI5 may well have been concerned about the lack of evidence against the IRA three if they were arrested 'prematurely' from MI5's point of view. Argument about the exact circumstances surrounding the death of the IRA team will continue. But one thing is certain: the SAS soldiers were heavily briefed by MI5 officers who told them they were following highly dangerous terrorists who could be expected to be ruthless and deadly if alerted to the fact that they were being followed. Anonymous MI5 officers, shielded from view, gave evidence at the inquest. But the jury was prevented from hearing crucial evidence about the MI5 operation and MI5's state of knowledge by public interest immunity certificates signed by government ministers. The MI5 officer in charge of the operation, the man who briefed the SAS soldiers, did not give evidence at all.

MI5 seems in effect to have misled the SAS into believing that the three IRA terrorists were armed and likely to be in possession of remote-control bomb detonators. It has also been pointed out that although the inquest was told the Spanish police had 'lost' the terrorists two days before the shooting, Spanish police were in fact asked by British security officials not to follow the gang on the morning of the shooting. And although the inquest was told by one officer that he alone assessed that the car contained a bomb, two other experienced army explosives officers were adamant there was no bomb. Neither of these two officers gave evidence at the inquest.[46]

A report by a legal observer on behalf of the National Council for Civil Liberties and the International League of Human Rights pointed to the limitations of the inquest and called for a public judicial inquiry into the shootings.[47] It is unlikely that the full story will ever come out, or official papers relating to the operation ever released.

## The Colin Wallace Affair

Colin Wallace, an army press officer in Northern Ireland in the mid-1970s, indulged in a disinformation exercise and psychological warfare. He alleges that MI5 officers in London supplied him by telex with material to build up a detailed dossier of British politicians, including their alleged personal and financial weaknesses.[48] The idea was to prepare propaganda for use against prominent Labour Party figures, including its leader Harold Wilson, as well as Liberal MPs and liberal Conservatives.

Wallace's plan, code-named 'Clockwork Orange', began as an attempt to combat terrorism by spreading disinformation in a way that would make extremist groups on both sides believe that they were infiltrated by informers. But the operation soon turned into a political one which reached its climax in the period between the two general elections of 1974. The Labour Party, Wallace alleges he was told by his MI5 contacts, promoted defence cuts, was anti-South African, soft on terrorism, and wanted to withdraw from the Common Market.

Using material supplied by MI5 officers in London, Wallace says he drew up reports claiming that up to 30 Labour MPs were secret members of the Communist Party, including Tony Benn, Ian Mikardo, Eric Heffer, Judith Hart, David Owen (the present SDP leader), Barbara Castle, Michael Foot and the late Tom Driberg and John Stonehouse. Wallace helped to forge documents purporting to show that Merlyn Rees, Labour's Northern Ireland Secretary, had contacts with Republican groups based in the US.

After he left Lisburn in 1975, Wallace provided material for Airey Neave MP, then a close political adviser of Mrs Thatcher and Conservative Spokesman on Northern Ireland. In August 1976 Neave responded to an approach from Wallace and told him in a letter: 'I read your material with great interest and wonder if it could be updated.'[49] Neave referred in particular to a forged document, *Ulster: A State of Subversion*, which purported to be an analysis of Soviet influence on Labour Party policies on Northern Ireland.

Wallace has also alleged that the security services were aware of child abuse taking place in the Kincora boys' home in east Belfast but took no action, so that they could use their knowledge to blackmail Loyalist politicians linked to the home. After an inquiry in 1980 – six years after Wallace first alerted the security services to the scandal – two members of an extreme Protestant sect, called Tara, were gaoled for abusing young boys. But three further inquiries, with limited terms of reference, failed to clear up the affair which at the time this book went to press remained a cause for concern.

Wallace was dismissed by Whitehall as a 'Walter Mitty' figure, acting on his own. Yet at the appeal against his sacking in 1975 – ostensibly for leaking information to a journalist in Belfast – his immediate superior in the Ministry of Defence press office in Lisburn, Peter Broderick, acknowledged that Wallace had been authorised to set up a covert 'psychological operations unit' despite misgivings in the Ministry of Defence in Whitehall. In 1981 Wallace was convicted of manslaughter in Arundel, West Sussex. He has always proclaimed his innocence.

Merlyn Rees, Northern Ireland Secretary at the time, has since said that he was unaware of these covert activities when he was in office. The disclosures, he has said, strengthen the case for an inquiry into what elements of MI5, including those described in *Spycatcher*, were up to in the 1970s.

After years of insisting that there was nothing in Wallace's allegations, the Government finally admitted in January 1990 that there had been a covert 'dirty tricks' campaign in Northern Ireland in the early and mid-1970s. It acknowledged the existence of the 'Clockwork Orange' propaganda aimed at extremist groups in Northern Ireland and the use of fake CIA cards and weapons in a hoax exercise. But, in a carefully-worded statement, it denied that propaganda was later aimed at mainland politicians. Ministers apologised for misleading MPs but also placed the blame on officials who had not told them the truth.[50]

The Government thus admitted the minimum it hoped it could get away with. It denied that there was any evidence that the security services were involved in a cover-up of homosexual abuse at Kincora. It also made no mention of Wallace's links with MI5. This was despite the fact that, for several months, senior Cabinet Office officials – including Sir Christopher Curwen, Thatcher's Intelligence and Security Co-ordinator and other members of the Joint Intelligence Committee – argued among themselves about what, if anything, they should disclose about Wallace's 'cover-job'. The Government agreed to a limited inquiry into the circumstances surrounding Wallace's dismissal in 1975, but at the time of writing, MPs on both sides of the Commons were still demanding a wider inquiry into the main allegation of an MI5 smear campaign against leading politicians.

## The Wilson Plot

Influential elements within MI5 (and the CIA) were hostile to the policies of Harold Wilson's Labour Governments. Prejudices and suspicions leading to what Peter Wright has called attempts to 'destabilise' the Wilson Government were stimulated by an imaginative Soviet defector, Anatoli Golitsin, who was managed by the notoriously conspiratorial head of the CIA's counter-espionage section, James 'Jesus' Angleton. Golitsin's claims led directly and indirectly to MI5 conducting three investigations into Wilson between 1963 and 1974. They found no evidence against him.

The first investigation was mounted after Golitsin claimed in 1963 that 'a Western opposition leader' was a Soviet agent. His claims were passed to MI5 just at the time when MI5 was looking into the strange death of Hugh Gaitskell, Wilson's predecessor, who had died of a rare disease, lupus disseminatus, shortly after a visit to the Soviet consulate where he had arranged to pick up a visa. Learning this, Golitsin told Sir Roger Hollis, then head of MI5, that he had heard in Moscow of a plan to assassinate 'some Western opposition leader'. MI5 opened a file on Wilson and found that he had made 17 trips to the Soviet Union, sometimes accompanied by his secretary, Marcia Williams (now Lady Falkender). Wilson was at the time sales representative of the timber merchants, Montagu Myers.[51]

According to David Leigh, author of *The Wilson Plot,* and other writers on the subject, the CIA claimed that it had new evidence against Wilson after he became Prime Minister in 1964. This turned out to be another source of Angleton's, a Soviet official in Mexico working for the CIA. The source, code-named 'Oatsheaf', said that Wilson was meeting with KGB agents. The third investigation into Wilson took place during Prime Minister Edward Heath's administration. A new Soviet defector, Oleg Lyalin, said he had been 'controlling' an agent who had social connections with Joseph Kagan (later ennobled and subsequently gaoled for tax frauds), an émigré textile merchant and one of Wilson's friends. The agent was a man called Vaygaukas, a member of the Soviet trade mission in London. Kagan was placed under surveillance by MI5 which, according to Peter Wright, tried to recruit agents in his Gannex coat factory near Leeds.

MI5, says Leigh, built up a file on Wilson, code-named 'Henry Worthington'. It was kept permanently in a safe in the Director-General's office.

Wright said in *Spycatcher* that from the late 1960s, some MI5 officers were encouraged to stir up trouble for Wilson. He alleged that Cecil King, chairman of the Mirror Group, whom he describes as a 'long time agent of ours', said he would readily publish stories inspired by MI5. Certainly King did attack the Labour Government with some vicious articles. It was part of King's campaign, Wright says, to bring down Labour and replace it with a national coalition led by Lord Mountbatten. Plots reached their peak, according to Wright, in 1974 with the election of a minority Labour administration. 'Wilson is a bloody menace', Wright recalls one of the younger MI5 officers as saying, 'and it's about time the public knew the truth.'[52] The idea, which Wright claims was supported by 30 senior officers (though he has since said only about half a dozen were involved and that he was the ringleader), was to work through smear campaigns and selective leaks to journalists hostile to the Government. According to Leigh, MI5 was alleged to have run a network of links with journalists including William Massie, defence correspondent of the *Sunday Express* and Jak (Raymond Jackson), the *Evening Standard* cartoonist.

Officers in MI5's K5 department bugged Marcia Williams, Wilson's political secretary. Its other targets included Lord Zuckerman, the Government's chief scientific adviser, and Robert Maxwell, the publisher and former Labour MP.[53]

## *The inquiries*

On two separate occasions in the autumn of 1974 Wilson warned his Cabinet colleagues of a smear campaign apparently conducted by elements within MI5. He was sufficiently concerned about what was going on that he called in Sir Maurice Oldfield, the head of MI6, to relay his suspicions. On August 7, 1975, he summoned the head of MI5, Sir Michael Hanley (who, ironically, was also at one time suspected by Wright and his so-called 'Young Turks' group of being a Soviet agent). Hanley, Wilson told the journalist Barrie Penrose, said to him that there had been a problem with a small right-wing faction in MI5 but that it had been solved.[54] Yet Thatcher told the Commons in 1987 that Hanley 'has categorically denied the allegation that he had confirmed the existence within the Security Service of a disaffected faction with extreme right wing views.'[55]

A first inquiry into the activities of Wright and his friends was undertaken by senior officers in MI5, apparently with a member of the Security Commission looking over their shoulder, when Callaghan took over from Wilson in 1976. In a letter to Wright dated August 2, 1976, after Wright had retired to Tasmania, Hanley wrote: 'It would take some imagination to say that things are improving here but they are certainly no worse than when you went away.' Hanley added in reference to the secret, internal, inquiry: 'The firm is doing quite well and passed the recent examinations.'[56]

In the aftermath of the *Spycatcher* affair, Mrs Thatcher told the Commons in May 1987 that she had asked the then Director-General of MI5, Sir Antony Duff, to investigate all the book's allegations. Despite the Worthington file, she said that there was no evidence of any plot or conspiracy against Wilson and that Duff had told her Wilson had 'never been the subject of a Security Service investigation or of any form of electronic or other surveillance'.[57] She said that MI5 officers in relevant posts at the time had been interviewed. However, one of the few named in *Spycatcher* – Harry Wharton – said later that he had not been interviewed.

Both Merlyn Rees and Lord Callaghan – the two former Labour ministers most directly involved in the limited 1977 inquiry and who were then responsible for MI5 – have since made it quite clear that their previous assumptions that all was well within MI5 in the 1970s may well have been misplaced. Both have called for a full-scale investigation into allegations of an MI5-based conspiracy against the 1974 Wilson Government. Lord Callaghan has said he is no longer confident that he had himself not misled the Commons in his 1977 statement in which he dismissed the allegations. As a result of their disquiet and their own experiences, both former ministers now support a system of independent oversight of MI5.[58]

## Other Labour suspects

Whatever the extent of a 'plot', Wilson believed that a section of the security and intelligence community was hostile to the democratically-elected government of the country. Wilson's former colleagues, Barbara Castle and Tony Benn, both recorded in their diaries that he was concerned about MI5's activities.

- Barbara Castle has explained that Wilson had a 'curious relationship' with the security services. He was deeply suspicious of them, but at the same time afraid of them, she said. This may also explain why he did not fight harder and ignore MI5's advice that Niall MacDermot, a rising star widely expected to become Solicitor-General, should not be promoted in 1968 from his post as Minister of State for Housing and Local Government. MacDermot told the author that he was targeted by MI5 on the grounds that his wife, Ludmila Benvenuto, an Italian resistance worker who helped in the escape of allied prisoners of war, was a security risk. He was questioned at length by MI5 officers. MacDermot says they refused to specify their concerns or the reasons for them. However, it was evident from their questions that the information MI5 had been given apparently included allegations that his wife had been a Communist. In fact, she had never been a member of the Italian or any other Communist Party.

- Judith (now Dame Judith) Hart, was refused security clearance by MI5 when Wilson wanted to appoint her Minister for Overseas Development in October 1974. MI5 told him it had 'documentary evidence' she had attended a Communist Party meeting in Poland. According to an article in *The Observer* in July 1977, the evidence was a newspaper cutting from the *Daily Worker* in 1950. The article described the visits of a British Communist delegation and was accompanied by a blurred photograph of a young woman laying a 'wreath for peace'. The caption named the woman as Mrs Tudor Hart – an Oxford academic. Yet the cutting had been placed in Judith Hart's MI5 file and had apparently remained there for over 20 years. At first, Wilson accepted MI5's veto and told Hart she could not be appointed. She finally got the post after Wilson, apparently convinced of her innocence, abruptly changed his mind. According to Joe Haines, Wilson's press secretary and now chief political editor of the Mirror Group, a telephone call made to Judith Hart after she became minister and intercepted by MI5 nearly cost her her job. It was only when a transcript was called for, he says, that it was found that she was merely pursuing an instruction from the National Executive of the Labour Party to find out what was happening in Chile.

- In 1974, Ted Short, now Lord Glenamara and then Labour's deputy leader, was a victim of a smear. The journalist, Chapman Pincher, was given a copy of a forged Swiss account claiming that Short was illegally investing in a foreign bank. Strict exchange controls were in place at the time. Lord Glenamara believes that the forged documents were part of a 'dirty campaign by people in MI5'.[59] An inquiry by Scotland Yard's serious crimes squad showed the documents to be highly professional forgeries, but not before they caused damageing publicity against Labour. Scotland Yard said it failed to track down the source. Lord Glenamara told the Labour MP, Tam Dalyell, that the police suddenly lost interest in the case.

- So little did Lord Gardiner trust the Security Service when he was Labour's Lord Chancellor that, he later confessed, he 'thought it more likely than not MI5 was bugging the telephones in my office'. When dealing with confidential business which concerned the Attorney-General, he would order his chauffeur to drive them round while they discussed it, confident, as he put it, 'she would never have allowed the car to be bugged without my knowledge'.[60]

## Foreign targets

Since the war MI5, with the help of MI6 and GCHQ, has monitored the activities and communications of foreign embassies in Britain while GCHQ and MI6 have also been involved in intelligence-gathering abroad. As Peter Wright has recorded, MI5 – helped by GCHQ – has bugged the Czech embassy, the Soviet consulate in Bayswater Road, and the Indonesian embassy.[61] Using a device which activated a telephone without anyone entering the premises, agents bugged Khrushchev's room at Claridge's Hotel in 1956. They bugged and read the ciphers of the Egyptian embassy in London throughout the Suez crisis that same year.

One of the most extensive bugging operations Wright says he helped to set up was in Lancaster House, off The Mall in London. The Foreign Office, which used the building for Commonwealth independence talks, agreed to the installation of a comprehensive covert microphone system. In the 1960s and 1970s it was used during all high-level negotiations, including the Zimbabwe independence talks.

MI5 and GCHQ have also bugged allied embassies. Prompted by MI6 and under pressure from the Foreign Office, they used the Post Office to get the plan of the French embassy's wiring. Between 1960 and 1963, according to Wright, they monitored every move the French made during the Macmillan Government's unsuccessful attempt to join the EC. As part of the operation, Britain passed to the United States details of French plans for de Gaulle's independent nuclear 'force de frappe'.

During the Suez crisis, the intelligence services were not content to bug the Egyptian embassy. Through GCHQ's listening post at Ayios Nikolaos in Cyprus, they picked up both Egyptian and Israeli communications. With the approval of the Prime Minister, Anthony Eden, MI6 plotted to assassinate President Nasser. But all of MI6's agents in the Egyptian army were discovered and arrested, and the plot collapsed. Another plan – to place canisters of nerve gas inside the ventilation system of Nasser's headquarters – never got beyond the planning stage.[62]

However, MI6 continued to indulge in violence in the Middle East. It helped to organise the coup in Abu Dhabi in 1967 when Sheikh Shakhbut was replaced by his brother Zaid. Concerned about the rebel movement in Oman in 1970, it succeeded with the help of British army units and the SAS in mounting a coup against the ageing Sultan, Said, and replacing him with his son, Qabous. After a successful attack on his palace, Said was flown to London where he was installed in the Dorchester Hotel.[63] In 1980, MI6 ran a destabilisation exercise in the Soviet-backed Marxist state of South Yemen, training rebels to blow up bridges and other installations.[64] MI6 also supplied weapons, including hand-held Blowpipe missile-launchers, to the rebel Mujahadeen in Afghanistan.[65]

The breadth of GCHQ's targeting and its implications for civil liberties and the integrity of international communications has already been noted. Its technological capacity does, however, bring rewards against specific terrorist targets (and the distinction between legitimate and illegitimate targets is crucial). For example, GCHQ first put MI5 on the trail of Nezar Hindawi, the Arab terrorist arrested in 1986 for attempting to place a bomb on an El Al airliner. GCHQ intercepted messages from the Syrian embassy in London to Syrian Air Force intelligence in Damascus in an operation that enabled Sir Geoffrey Howe, the then foreign secretary, to speak of 'conclusive evidence' of Syrian involvement with Hindawi.[66]

# CHAPTER SEVEN

# How Others Do It

Whitehall's sensitivity to any public discussion – let alone independent accountability – of Britain's security and intelligence agencies, is unique. Britain's longest-standing allies in the world of security and intelligence – the US, Canada and Australia – have all introduced a system of democratic accountability following the exposure of scandals similar to those exposed in Britain.

We will look at the US first, not because it offers Britain the best lessons, but because it is the most powerful western nation and at the same time the most open society. If there is a lesson to be learned from the US it is that despite a powerful Congress jealous of its authority, the executive, as Irangate demonstrated, will continue to bypass even the most comprehensive procedures designed to ensure that it is held to account to the elected legislature. We will then look at the situation in Canada and Australia, two countries whose constitutions are based on the Westminster model and whose experience cannot be met with the objection – frequently made by Whitehall in relation to US practice – that Britain has nothing to learn from foreign experience because the constitutional set-up is so different from the British tradition. But first we will briefly look at the situation in Western Europe in the run up to 1992.

## Western Europe

Countries throughout Western Europe have established procedures for subjecting their security services to some form of democratic scrutiny, and their activities are limited by constitutional safeguards. The security and intelligence services of most Western European countries have to account to parliamentary committees for their expenditure and spell out their outlook, priorities and major operations. The heads of the agencies are well-known figures who are often ready to explain their tasks and problems in public. Some agencies – the West German and Italian equivalents of MI5, for example – publish annual reports with details of their target groups, the extent to which they are considered to pose a threat and the numbers of their members.

### *1992*

The dawning of 1992 – the year by which European Community countries have pledged themselves to break down all frontier controls on the movement of capital, goods and people – has implications for intra-agency co-operation. The security services of EC states already meet regularly under the aegis of the so-called Trevi Group – informal meetings of EC interior ministers. West Germany and Spain have now proposed setting up some kind of EC-wide FBI. The Bonn Government has suggested a system of shared responsibilities whereby one country would collect information on firearms, for example, while another would maintain a European Community database on the identification of suspected terrorists. Bonn has also proposed the introduction of a 'search for priority targets' whereby photographs and detailed descriptions of targets would be distributed to all EC police forces.

Britain is less than enthusiastic about these plans. It told its EC partners that the distribution of such information was dangerous 'because some of the information is obtained from sensitive sources such as informants or surveillance photographs'.[1] The British police are as wary as the Government about the implications of 1992. The Association of Chief Police Officers has publicly opposed the European Commission's proposals – backed by most member countries – to remove internal EC frontier controls. Frank Jordan, Chief Constable of Kent, told a House of Lords committee that removing border controls would 'substantially impair' efforts against terrorism.[2]

But one thing is clear: with an increasingly integrated Europe, citizens and parliaments of Britain's EC partners are likely to demand more effective safeguards and monitoring methods. It will be difficult for Whitehall to ignore this.

## *West Germany*

The West German experience offers some instances of openness which, though modest, would send shivers through Whitehall if practised in Britain. Early in 1988, for example, Christian Lochte, the chief official in Hamburg of the Bundesamt fur Verfassungsschutz (BfV) – which literally means 'the Federal Office for the Protection of the Constitution' – publicly called for a dialogue with terrorists. Young people who joined the Red Army Faction – the successor to the Baader-Meinhof group – changed their politics as time went on, he said.

Later in the same year Lochte accused the police of 'data mania' and said that only one-fifth of computer information collected on alleged left-wing terrorists was relevant. He disclosed in a legal gazette that federal police computers had stored information on 3,000 alleged terrorists and another 11,000 supporters. Police theories about 'preventive measures' to combat terrorism had reached 'fantastic proportions', he said, and claimed that in many cases legal principles had been ignored.[3]

In August 1988 the head of the BfV, Gerhard Boeden, told the *Financial Times* in an interview – itself something that would be unthinkable in Britain – that his agency, the equivalent of Britain's MI5, should learn from the lessons of the past. 'Our citizens should know that this institution was founded, after our bitter experiences, to protect one of the most liberal constitutions that Germany has ever had, from a situation where political forces – either from the right or the left – could try to abolish parliamentary democracy.'[4]

It is true that West Germany is uniquely sensitive about its past, illustrated by its 'Berufsverbot' vetting system in effect requiring public sector employees to place loyalty to the state and the constitution above personal conscience. But it has also been particularly vulnerable to the threat of spies infiltrating from the East. Despite this, however, the BfV has not retreated behind a screen of silence. It even publishes a brochure, translated into English, explaining its guidelines. Under the heading, 'Intelligence Methods', it says these include: 'The infiltration or recruitment and handling of agents in extremist or terrorist organisations; the surveillance of suspects; secret photography; interception of post and telecommunications; other measures to conceal certain BfV operational activity by the use of non-attributable vehicle registration numbers or identity cards with cover names.'[5] This may all be thoroughly unsurprising and part of the attempt to conjure an avuncular image but it is still something MI5 refuses to acknowledge, either to MPs or to the public.

Similarly, while the Government continues to maintain the fiction that Sir Colin McColl and his organisation, MI6, does not officially exist, his French opposite number has given an extensive interview to the French newspaper, *Le Monde*.[6]

## Eastern Europe

Security services have been a central target in the constitutional and political upheavals in Eastern Europe and it is certain that in most countries they will be subjected to some kind of democratic scrutiny in the future.

Indications are that the security services of Eastern Europe will be based on West Germany's BfV, a more open and accountable model than its British counterpart. Significantly, Istvan Horvath, the Hungarian Interior Minister, resigned in January 1990 over a disclosure that the security service had bugged opposition leaders. The scandal was sparked off by a leak from a security official to the opposition, which was later told by a security source that the security service had also shredded documents about the surveillance of banks, universities, companies and foreign embassies. It is unthinkable that a senior official, let alone a minister, would resign over a similar incident in Britain.

## The European Convention on Human Rights

To date, the greatest pressure for change in the way the British security services operate has come not from other European countries but from the European Convention on Human Rights, which was drawn up by the Council of Europe in 1950. The Convention establishes a right to privacy (Article 8) and – more importantly in this context – a right to an 'effective remedy' in domestic law against possible breaches of the Convention (Article 13). As we have seen, the Government believes that the Security Service Act meets its European obligations. As soon as the Bill was published it sent a copy to the European Commission on Human Rights which had recently said that the Government had a case to answer in the Harman-Hewitt case brought by *Liberty*.

There are, however, serious doubts as to whether the Act *does* provide the 'effective remedy' for aggrieved persons that the European Court has in past cases ruled that national governments must provide. As explained, the shortcomings of the Security Service Act revolve around the limited role and functions of the commissioner and the tribunal, the extent of the discretionary powers enjoyed by MI5 and the fact that warrants are issued without any judicial authority. These issues were highlighted in two cases that have come before the European Court.

## *The Leander case*

Torsten Leander, a Swedish carpenter, was sacked from his job at the country's Naval Museum after he failed security vetting. He was given no reason for the decision. The European Court stated in its 1987 judgment that it had to be satisfied that 'adequate and effective safeguards' against abuse existed because of the potential risk to democracy of secret surveillance. By a majority it ruled that, taken together, the remedies and safeguards established in Sweden satisfied the Convention on Human Rights although, on their own, each would have been inadequate. The safeguards included:

- the presence of MPs on the National Police Board which operates Sweden's security and intelligence records;
- the active engagement of the Minister of Justice and Chancellor of Justice in supervising and monitoring the activities of the board;
- a parliamentary ombudsman who can investigate individual complaints and has access to documents and files in order to do so;
- the existence of a parliamentary committee on justice, consisting of 15 MPs, which has the power to inquire into the activities of the security and intelligence agencies with full access to their registers.

The European Court said it attached 'particular importance to the presence of parliamentarians' on the National Police Board and the Parliamentary Justice Committee. As we have seen, MPs in Britain have no role under the Security Service Act. The Court also stated that to justify interference with a person's right to privacy on national security grounds, there must be 'an adequate indication of the scope and manner of the exercise of the discretion conferred on the responsible authorities to collect, record and release information...' The law, it added, 'has to be sufficiently clear in its terms to give ordinary citizens an adequate indication as to the circumstances in which and the conditions on which the public authorities are empowered to resort to secret and potentially dangerous interference with private life.'[7] The Security Service Act fails these tests.

## *The Klass Case*

Five West German lawyers claimed that legislation allowing their government to open mail and tap telephones was in breach of the European Convention on Human Rights. They, too, lost the case. However, in its judgment in 1978, the Court noted that the minister responsible had to report at least every six months to an all-party committee. Independent scrutiny was required, the Court said, 'in a field where abuse is potentially so easy in individual cases and could have such harmful consequences for democratic society as a whole.' The Court noted that under Article 8 of the Convention, powers of secret surveillance of citizens, 'characterising as they did the police state', were tolerable only insofar as 'strictly necessary' to safeguard democratic institutions.[8]

Governments, the Court added, could not enjoy unlimited discretion in subjecting their citizens to secret surveillance and warned of the dangers of laws undermining or even destroying democracy on the grounds of defending it. There must be 'adequate and effective guarantees against abuse'.[9] In Germany, it noted, individuals could complain to an independent commission and the Constitutional Court. The commission has the authority to order the minister to inform an individual that s/he has been subjected to secret surveillance. In addition, an official 'qualified for judicial office' examines the information obtained by surveillance before passing it to the security services to ensure that it is relevant to the reasons given for acquiring it. The security services are also under a duty to inform the target as soon as surveillance is ended and he or she can be told without jeopardising the purpose of the surveillance. The essential differences between West German practice and the British system is the absence in this country of any parliamentary scrutiny or recourse to the courts.

## The United States

US security and intelligence agencies, like all the other arms of the executive, have from the outset been subject to Congressional oversight. That, anyway, is the theory enshrined in the American Constitution.

### *The Central Intelligence Agency*

The CIA was established in 1947 by the National Security Act (which also set up the National Security Council to which the CIA is officially responsible).

The 1947 National Security Act laid down statutory restrictions on domestic telephone-tapping and the interception of mail. In Congress, the CIA was the responsibility of intelligence sub-committees of the Senate and House of Representatives armed forces committees. Its budget had to be approved by Congress and monitored by the General Accounting Office, akin to Britain's National Audit Office under the Comptroller and Auditor-General.

These sub-committees met in secret and scrutiny of the CIA was haphazard and inconsistent. The CIA gave little information about its activities and Congress rarely pressed for more. The traditional Congress attitude was expressed by Senator Leverett Saltonstall of Massachusetts in 1956:

> It is not a question of reluctance on the part of CIA officials to speak to us. Instead, it is a question of our reluctance, if you will, to seek information and knowledge on subjects which I, personally, as a member of Congress and as a citizen, would rather not have, unless I believed it to be my responsibility to have it because it might involve the lives of American citizens.[10]

### *The Federal Bureau of Investigation*

Unlike the CIA, the FBI, set up in 1935, has no charter. The director answers to the attorney-general. But three committees of each House of Congress have an oversight role: the two Appropriations and Intelligence Committees in each House of Congress and, in addition, a sub-committee of the Judiciary Committee (in the Senate) and the Civil and Constitutional Rights sub-committee (in the House of Representatives).

The latter is currently chaired by an ex-FBI agent called Don Edwards who has lost nothing of his former investigative zeal. For example, he vigorously pursued evidence that the FBI had penetrated anti-Contra groups with the result that the agents involved were disciplined.

The FBI also sends an annual report of its activities to Congress. These reports are the basis of the Agency's budget request and the raw material on which the director and Department of Justice officials are questioned by the

Congress Appropriation Committees. They contain 150 pages of information, ranging from police training and civil rights issues to drugs and terrorism.

## *Proposals for reform*

It was not until the late 1960s and early 1970s that public and Congressional attention began to focus on the activities of the CIA (and, in its wake, the FBI), following the exposure, mainly in the press, about covert action in Chile, Cambodia and elsewhere, and of large-scale CIA spying activities on American citizens in the US. The American press disclosed that the CIA had kept secret dossiers on US citizens, had infiltrated groups opposed to the administration's policies, such as the Vietnam war, had engaged in illegal wire-taps and intercepted mail. Although neither the CIA nor the FBI was directly involved, Watergate confirmed suspicions that America's security and intelligence apparatus was out of control. Attempts in the 1950s, 60s, and early 70s to set up permanent, specialist, intelligence committees had all been defeated – Watergate changed the environment.

The Commission on CIA Activities within the USA, set up by President Ford in the wake of Nixon's downfall after the Watergate revelations, noted in 1975 that 'the role of the (existing) sub-committees has generally been to exert policy-making influence informally through personal discussions with the Director of Central Intelligence.'[11] The Church Committee on Intelligence, set up by the Senate the same year, said 'Congress has failed to provide the necessary statutory guidelines to ensure that intelligence agencies carry out their missions in accord with constitutional process.'[12]

The Church investigations, which produced ten volumes of evidence and comment, concluded that the 1947 National Security Act was no longer an adequate framework for the conduct of America's intelligence activities. The Committee commented that neither espionage, covert action nor paramilitary warfare is explicitly authorised by the 1947 Act, yet these have come to be major activities conducted by the Central Intelligence Agency operating at the direction of the President through the National Security Council.

Church blamed past presidents for failing to exercise adequate control over intelligence activities and prevent abuses. 'In essence', the Committee concluded, 'presidents have not exercised effective oversight.'[13]

Furthermore, the secrecy surrounding the intelligence budget made it impossible for 'Congress as a whole to make use of this valuable oversight tool'. Funds for the CIA, NSA and the defence intelligence agencies had been concealed in the Pentagon budget.

Senator Walter Mondale, the former Democrat presidential candidate and a member of the Church Committee, summarised what it had discovered in a lecture to the Kansas Law School in November 1976:

Our investigations showed that many of the abuses of the Nixon years could be traced back to the attitudes of the Cold War.

Fastened on us was the fearful myth that America could not be defended without more deceit and illegality than democracy permits – and without more cynicism and hypocrisy than our beliefs would allow.

For years, this assumption was used to justify actions abroad – from subversion of freely elected governments, to assassination attempts aimed at foreign leaders. And inevitably, in Macbeth's words, the invention returned home 'to plague the inventor'.

The CIA came home to launch 'operation chaos' – a surveillance programme directed against American citizens – even though that agency is forbidden from exercising internal security functions. The law didn't matter.

The army spied on the lawful democratic activities of groups ranging across the political spectrum – from Carl McIntyre's Conservative Christian Action Movement and the John Birch Society to the Urban Coalition, the Anti-Defamation League and even the Chamber of Commerce. The law didn't matter.

There was massive invasion of privacy. For years the FBI and the CIA illegally tapped phones and engaged in other forms of electronic surveillance. The law didn't matter.

The FBI and CIA both opened the private mail of American citizens. Over 300,000 first class letters were opened – the mail of people like John Steinbeck, Senators Church and Kennedy, and organisations like the Federation of American Scientists. The law didn't matter.

The National Security Agency obtained from major international cable companies copies of all private telegrams sent overseas by American citizens or businesses. The law didn't matter.

Legitimate law-enforcement functions were twisted and perverted. In 1969 the Internal Revenue Service established a 'Special Services Staff' to examine the tax returns of individuals – not because they had violated the tax laws, but because some people in government did not like their politics. The law didn't matter.

> Eventually these agencies resorted to the Commission of Common Crimes to obtain what they considered necessary information. So the FBI and the CIA illegally broke into the homes and businesses of American citizens – the so called 'black bag jobs'. They even established official liaison with organised crime. The law didn't matter.
>
> Perhaps the most terrifying abuse of power during this period was what the FBI called Cointelpro. That ugly little acronym would have been at home in any police state in Eastern Europe or Latin America; it meant illegal investigations targeted against American law-abiding individuals in groups – and punishment administered not by a court but by a government agency – through harassment and tactics designed to break up marriages, destroy reputations, terminate employment, sabotage political campaigns and even encourage violent retribution by falsely and anonymously labelling intended victims as government informers.[14]

The Church Committee uncovered the CIA's covert use of academics, publications, students and trade union organisations. President Ford's Commission found that the CIA had kept records on American citizens which were not needed for 'legitimate or security purposes', had helped the police to monitor anti-war demonstrations and provided classified information to Nixon on the Bay of Pigs fiasco, the Cuban missile crisis and the Vietnam war which was used to serve the President's personal political ends. Although there is no evidence that the CIA participated in the Watergate conspiracy or the subsequent cover-up, it had provided material to a conspirator and destroyed files during the investigations following the Watergate arrests.

## *Statutory controls*

Ford's Commission, the Church Committee and investigations by the press heralded a new array of statutory controls over the US intelligence agencies. In 1978 Congress passed the Foreign Intelligence Surveillance Act (FISA). It set out to control wire-taps and other forms of electronic surveillance inside the US, stating that the CIA and other intelligence agencies had to use the 'least intrusive' techniques and seek only genuine information – and that there had to be cause to believe that the US citizen placed under surveillance was an agent of a foreign power. The attorney-general would have to agree to a certificate which would then be passed to a special court meeting in secret. As far as is known, the court, comprising federal judges chosen by the Chief Justice, has never refused a certificate under the Act.

A Presidential Order in 1980 went further, dividing the responsibilities of the CIA and the FBI as recommended by President Ford's Commission, the Church Committee and the Pike Committee of the House of Representatives (which had conducted a parallel inquiry to Church's). It ruled that the CIA could not conduct any electronic surveillance inside the US; though it could initiate requests under the FISA, it had to hand over the operation to the FBI once the special court had given its clearance. But no TV surveillance, mail interception or house searches could be conducted without specific permission from the attorney-general.

These individual reforms culminated in the 1980 Intelligence Oversight Act which formally established the pre-eminent position of Congress by setting up permanent intelligence committees – one for the Senate and one for the House of Representatives.

The two committees have 15 members each and are supported by a large staff. Both the committee members and their staff are vetted. They have a right to call for any people or papers they wish. The committees are to be kept 'fully and currently informed of all intelligence activities ... including any significant anticipated intelligence activity'.[15] It is illegal for an agency not to disclose to Congress any operation, however covert (except for names, dates and places).

In practice, details of sensitive operations continue to be withheld although the principle that Congress must be informed sooner or later about all operations has been firmly established. As a way to get round the practical difficulties, Congress passed a new amendment allowing the intelligence agencies to inform the chairmen of the committees and the senior minority members privately before undertaking sensitive operations. Congress has in general accepted that it cannot receive prior notification of all covert CIA operations. But it expects the President to inform the committees in due course: in this respect it has to rely on trust.

The Senate select committee on intelligence was established 'to oversee and make continuing studies of the intelligence activities and programmes of the United States Government' and 'to provide vigilant legislative oversight over the intelligence activities of the United States to ensure that such activities are in conformity with the constitution and laws of the United States.'[16] It can report its findings and proposals for legislation to the full Senate.

The select committee covers 'the intelligence activities' of all government departments and agencies, including the CIA, the Pentagon, the State Department and the FBI, which are also obliged to send the committee an annual report. An unclassified version of the report is published at the committee's discretion.

There are a number of provisos designed to protect the secrecy of sensitive information. The names of individuals engaged in intelligence activities are protected, as are intelligence methods and the sources of information on which the annual reports are based. No staff member or adviser to the committee can be shown classified information unless s/he agrees under oath to abide by the rules of the Senate and has been given a security clearance by the director of the CIA.

The intelligence committees – and Congress as a whole – hold to the fundamental principle that they should be given, and be trusted with, all the information they ask for. The Senate intelligence committee, for example, decides whether to disclose classified information given to it by the government in private if, in its view, it is in the public interest to do so. But there are elaborate procedures designed to avoid conflict and embarrassment and to ensure that leaks do not take place.

Before disclosing information given to it in private, the committee has first to notify the president (who also has the right to nominate a liaison officer who can attend any closed meeting of the committee). The president has to notify the committee of any objections to disclosure within five days; the committee can then put the matter to the full Senate, which then debates the issue in closed session. The Senate has the final say in deciding whether or not information should be revealed. Leaks from the intelligence committees are taken seriously. A leak could lead to the expulsion from the Senate of the offending individual and sacking in the case of a staff member.

Almost identical procedures and membership rules cover the activities of the House of Representatives intelligence committee.

Thick, sealed doors, protected by armed guards, show the extent to which the committees are determined to protect the secrets which the government shares with them. There is a widespread view that Congressmen have responded to their privileged position by tending to 'overcompensate' – by being more secretive than they need to be.[17]

There is also a procedure designed to inform the president – as opposed to Congress – about the agencies' activities. This is done through the Intelligence Oversight Board (IOB), consisting of outsiders such as lawyers, academics, scientists and electronics experts. Covert operations require the president's specific authorisation or, in special circumstances, approval soon after the event. The president's executive orders are monitored by the IOB, which clears them before they are published.

## *Freedom of information*

All American security and intelligence agencies are covered by the Freedom of Information Act (FOI) passed in 1966, with amendments added in 1974 when

– after exposures that the agencies had engaged in questionable and sometimes unlawful activities – Congress also passed a Privacy Act. There are exemptions to disclosure, notably covering information which in the view of the executive must be kept secret 'in the interest of national defence or foreign policy'. However, individuals or groups refused information can appeal to the courts.

Disclosures under the FOI Act revealed that the FBI and other federal agencies had gathered a massive number of files on over 100 American writers, including Ernest Hemingway, John Steinbeck, Pearl Buck, Thomas Wolfe and William Faulkner. Much of the information was found to be factually inaccurate, sometimes alleging crimes by innuendo or guilt by association.

Penn Kimball, a former journalist, discovered in 1978 through the FOI and Privacy Acts that the CIA, FBI, and State Department had accumulated secret files on him. He was classified as a 'dangerous national security risk'. One file recorded that he was once seen drinking in the company of an alleged Communist and another that he was overheard in the corridors of *Time* magazine saying something favourable about Tito. In his account of his ten-year struggle to clear his name he described how he met bureaucratic obstacles familiar anywhere in the world.[18] He noted that the Privacy Act gives US citizens the right to retrieve records kept on them by federal agencies, though with exemptions. 'Among the authorised deletions', he said, 'are the names of confidential informants, clues which might help you to guess who they are, and material which, if released, would be deemed harmful to national security.' You need 'staying power', he commented, to exercise your rights.[19] Some of his files, when released, were heavily annotated, with sections censored. This puts America's reputation for 'openness' in perspective. Nevertheless, he was at least able to know of the existence of the files; in Britain the struggle could not even begin. No one here has the right to ask for, let alone see, files held on them by the security and intelligence services.[20]

## Canada

Evidence of abuse of power and growing public unease have persuaded the Canadian government to introduce sweeping reforms and controls over the country's security and intelligence services. As in Australia (and Britain) concern was focused on activities directed against 'subversion'. As in Australia (but not Britain), the government abandoned the term 'subversion' in 1988 as being too vague in what was anyway considered a grey area.

### *Proposals for reform*

Pressure for reform grew in 1976 after a former constable in the Royal Canadian Mounted Police (RCMP) was brought to trial on charges relating to the bombing of a private residence. He testified that he had done 'much worse things'. Official assurances that this was an 'isolated incident' were soon dismissed in the wake of further evidence that the security services had broken into the homes of members of the separatist movement in Quebec and left-wing groups.

As a result, the government set up a Royal Commission under Mr Justice McDonald in 1977. The Commission's report, *Freedom and Security Under the Law*, remains a seminal work on the role of security services in a democratic society.[21] It proposed a wide range of recommendations which, sooner or later, were to be accepted by the government. It laid down five basic principles which, it said, should govern the Canadian Security Intelligence Service (CSIS): the rule of law is paramount; the means of investigation must be proportionate to the gravity of the threat; the need for investigative techniques must be weighed against the damage they might do to personal freedom and privacy; the more intrusive the technique, the higher the authority required to approve its use; except in emergencies, less intrusive techniques must be preferred to more intrusive ones. To begin with, it said, responsibility for security and intelligence-gathering should be taken away from the RCMP.[22]

## *Statutory controls*

In 1984 an Act of Parliament set up a separate agency, CSIS, with an inspector-general (IG) and an independent review committee to monitor its activities. The CSIS itself was put under the control of the solicitor-general, who has the responsibility of drawing up directives for the head of CSIS. These directives cover guidelines on the principles and policies governing the conduct of CSIS investigations and the scope and intensity of 'the security intelligence net' – its targets. Directives issued to the director-general of CSIS – who cannot hold office for more than 10 years – must be disclosed to parliament and to the CSIS Review Committee.

Applications for warrants 'to investigate a threat to the security of Canada' have to be approved by the solicitor-general and made to a judge in writing. The CSIS has to state in an affidavit that other investigatory methods have been tried and failed and that telephone-tapping, bugging, mail interception or house searches are necessary. The affidavit has to describe 'the type of communication proposed to be intercepted, the type of information, records, documents or things proposed to be obtained', and the identity of the target.[23]

Section 2(d) of the Act states that the CSIS can collect, analyse and retain information which 'may on reasonable grounds be suspected of constituting threats to the security of Canada' but only to the extent that it is 'strictly necessary'. 'Threats to the security of Canada' include acts of espionage or sabotage, 'foreign influenced activities ... detrimental to the interests of Canada', 'clandestine or deceptive' activities supporting the threat or use of 'serious violence against persons or property for the purpose of achieving a political objective', and 'covert unlawful' activities aimed at 'the destruction or overthrow by violence of the constitutionally established system of government in Canada'.[24] This is a much tighter definition than that used by the British government, and the Act explicitly excludes 'lawful advocacy, protest or dissent' from the agency's mandate. Yet even this definition has been criticised by the CSIS review committee as being too ambiguous.

The IG sees all the reports sent to the solicitor-general by the head of CSIS. He then submits a certificate to the solicitor-general in which he states whether or not, in his view, CSIS has disobeyed or ignored ministerial directives or indulged in 'an unreasonable or unnecessary exercise' of its powers.[25] Both the CSIS reports and the certificates are passed to the Security Intelligence Review Committee (SIRC).

This Committee consists of between three and five members, all privy councillors but not members of the Senate or the House of Commons. They are appointed by the governor-general after consulting the prime minister and leaders of all the parties which have at least 12 MPs in the Commons (see Appendix IV).

The SIRC has an extremely wide mandate. It can question ministerial directives to CSIS as well as reports sent to the government by the CSIS director-general. It can conduct an inquiry whether the solicitor-general wants it to or not. It can direct the CSIS or the IG to conduct an investigation into a particular matter. The Committee, which can also seek the advice of Canada's Human Rights Commission, is entitled to have access to any information 'it deems necessary for the performance of its duties and functions'.[26]

In addition, any Canadian citizen may make a complaint to the Committee about 'any act or thing done by the service'.[27] It can investigate the complaint so long as the individual concerned has already made a direct approach to the CSIS but has not, in the Committee's view, received a satisfactory response. The Committee has to satisfy itself that the complaint is not 'trivial, frivolous, vexatious or made in bad faith'.[28] Complaints can relate to alleged violations of Canada's immigration laws and Human Rights Act as well as the CSIS. The Committee can also make complaints on behalf of individuals – civil servants, for example, or defence contractors – who have been denied security clearance. Investigations into complaints are conducted in private; but the Committee has the power to subpoena witnesses and oblige them to give evidence on oath. It can hear evidence and seek information whether or not they would be admissible in a court of law.

Every three months the CSIS gives the Committee figures on the number of warrants issued, the individuals or groups which have been targeted and the reasons why. (The Committee has said that the solicitor-general should consider whether there ought to be what it calls a 'devil's advocate' to argue the case against a warrant.)

The Committee also monitors mail-opening and CSIS expenditure. It gives evidence to the Commons Standing Committee on Terrorism and Public Safety, as does the CSIS director. It has the right of access to all information in the hands of the CSIS other than 'cabinet confidences'. It is itself answerable to the Federal Court of Appeal.

The CSIS, which has a 'Media Relations Unit', is also covered by Canada's Access to Information, Human Rights and Privacy Acts.[29] Relatively few requests have been tabled under the former – about 150 under the latter – and the legislation allows the agency to refuse to acknowledge the existence of certain categories of files. (Disagreement, however, can lead to appeals to the country's Information Commissioner.)

There was one recommendation from the McDonald Commission which the government did not accept; this was the proposal that there should be direct parliamentary oversight of the CSIS, through a committee with members from both the Senate and the Commons. Politics in Canada are fiercely partisan and both the government and the intelligence bureaucracy were terrified of leaks.

## *Abolition of the Counter-Subversion Branch*

The activities of the CSIS Counter-Subversion Branch began to cause concern to the Review Committee in the 1980s. The Committee made its fears known in a hard-hitting annual report for the year 1986-87.

The flavour of the report is reflected in its choice for its frontispiece of the familiar quote from Juvenal: '*Quis custodiet ipsos custodes?*' ('Who is to guard the guards themselves?') In the 1986-87 report the Committee described its mandate as ensuring that the Canadian Security and Intelligence Service carries out its work effectively but 'without reasonable or unnecessary intrusions on individual rights'.

With a logic that has evaded successive British governments, it added: '*because of* its wide powers of investigation and the secrecy that unavoidably surrounds much of its work, CSIS comes under a variety of controls, both judicial and administrative' (our emphasis). It also said: 'We believe that in a healthy democracy there can and should be a degree of informed public discussion on national security issues.'[30]

In that year (1986-87) the Committee made nearly 150 formal inquiries to the CSIS. They included some prompted by press reports – for example, stories about alleged fund-raising for Contra rebels in Nicaragua, recruiting by the white-supremacist organisation Aryan Nation, alleged surveillance of a peace activist who had met a suspected Soviet agent, and immigration applications from people alleged to have been involved in torture and murder in Chile.

But the Committee's main concern were the activities of the CSIS Counter-Subversion Branch and the criteria it used for targeting. It found that entire categories of people were targeted – the complete membership of a particular group, for example, even though only a few might (publicly) have advocated violence and even though there was no evidence of any covert foreign influence (the two criteria most often cited). Targeting by category, it said, 'takes insufficient account of potential harm to the principles of personal freedom and privacy'.[31]

Recognising the real threats posed by a few organisations, the Committee nevertheless judged that the CSIS was spending money and effort on too many counter-espionage targets and 'intruding on the lives and activities of too many Canadians in this area'. After reviewing CSIS operational files on five organisations representing different categories of counter-subversion targets, the Committee concluded that the Counter-Subversion Branch was concerned primarily with two things – the potential for foreign powers to manipulate Canadian policy through legitimate protest groups, and the possibility that certain groups might undermine Canadian institutions and bring about the violent overthrow of the state.

In a stinging aside, it said that in both cases there appeared to be an underlying belief that the Canadian public was 'only too liable to be duped'. The CSIS, the Committee commented, over-estimated the influence and persuasive power of these groups, adding: 'From our own reading of the media and our own personal knowledge of people in every walk of life, we know that Canadians are generally mature enough to resist the blandishment of the groups concerned.' It was possible, it said, that any targeted group could undertake terrorist acts at some point, but on the available evidence most were unlikely to do so in the foreseeable future.[32]

These observations led the Review Committee to come to the conclusion that the CSIS Counter-Subversion Branch should be dismantled. The main cause was the practice of targeting groups rather than individuals – an individual became a target simply because he or she was a member of a particular organisation deemed to be subversive. As we have seen, this procedure is specifically sanctioned in the British Security Service Act.

In 1988, the Canadian government accepted the Review Committee's proposal and said its residual role should be transferred to the CSIS Counter-Terrorism and Counter-Intelligence branches. The government announced that the number of individuals targeted by the Counter-Subversion Branch had already been reduced by 95 percent since 1981 and that any remaining targets – mainly groups – would in future be watched by the CSIS

Analysis and Production Branch which uses only open, non-intrusive information-collection methods.[33]

Meanwhile, evidence that independent oversight does have real bite was dramatically demonstrated in 1987 when the CSIS director resigned after evidence in a court case that the agency had wrongfully obtained a warrant to target an individual.

## Australia

Every year the director-general (DG) of the Australian Security Intelligence Organisation (ASIO), the equivalent of Britain's MI5, publishes a report outlining its activities and main preoccupations over the past 12 months. The first of its 40 or so pages contains a covering letter signed by the DG to the responsible minister, the attorney-general. In Britain, by comparison, even the name of the head of MI5 is not officially acknowledged.

ASIO's annual report explains the agency's legislative basis, gives an outline of its intelligence methods and priorities, and details of its budget and organisational structure. It includes a summary of how ASIO is held to account and the system of ministerial responsibility. Remarkably – for a British audience – the report contains the telephone numbers of ASIO headquarters and of its regional offices in the different Australian states. The latest annual report, covering the year 1986-87, records that the DG gave a number of interviews to the media and addressed the National Press Club in Canberra, where he also responded to questions from journalists. In a book published in Australia in the summer of 1988, Harvey Barnett, a former DG of ASIO, wrote: 'Officers are trained to explain themselves to the general public, stressing that they work under the authority of Parliament as expressed by the ASIO Act.'[34]

### *Proposals for reform*

ASIO was set up with help from MI5 in 1949 after the US expressed concern about the potential danger of sharing secrets with Australia, a country which at that time had no national security service or vetting system. Britain was eager to help, particularly since it was planning nuclear weapons tests in Australia.

Demand for stricter formal controls over ASIO came with the election of a Labor government under Gough Whitlam in 1972. Labor's mistrust of the security and intelligence services, built up over 23 years in opposition, led to calls at the Party's conference in 1972 for an inquiry into the intelligence community. The government set up a Royal Commission on Australia's Security and Intelligence Agencies (RCASIA) under Justice Hope, a New South Wales Appeal Court judge and former president of the Australian Council of Civil Liberties. Hope completed his report in 1977, by which time Malcolm Fraser's

Liberal-National Party coalition was in power. But the new government happily accepted Hope's proposals and introduced the 1979 ASIO Act as a result. It included tighter controls over telephone-taps and bugging devices (which require the personal sanction of the attorney-general) an annual report to Parliament, tighter definitions of 'subversion', controls over targeting of individuals, and a less 'paternalistic' style of management. Hope had also proposed that the leader of the opposition should also be consulted on security matters (including the appointment of the director-general of ASIO), and be provided with a copy of the organisation's unabridged annual report. Fraser accepted Hope's proposal for an Office of National Assessment, independent of all other government departments and agencies, to provide ministers with up-to-date intelligence assessments, analysis and research. Fraser also accepted Whitlam's choice of Edward Woodward, a federal High Court judge, to head ASIO.

The 1979 ASIO Act also established a Security Appeals Tribunal under a senior judge whereby individuals can challenge security assessments of themselves which they believe are unfair or based on inaccuracies. In 1983 the tribunal delivered what former head of ASIO Harvey Barnett described as a 'watershed' judgment.[35] A member of the Communist Party of Australia (CPA), Stephen Rix, was being interviewed for a job in the Department of Trade and Resources where he would be required to have access to secret information. ASIO advised that Rix should be denied access to national secrets because of his CPA membership. The tribunal ruled that membership of the CPA in itself was not, under the terms of the 1979 ASIO Act, a reason for being denied access to classified material.

Nevertheless, latent suspicions in the Australian Labor Party (ALP) about ASIO were fuelled by continuing allegations in the press and, in particular, by the Combe/Ivanov affair which broke shortly after Labor was returned to power in 1983. David Combe, a former national secretary of the ALP, was approached by Valery Ivanov, a secretary in the Soviet embassy in Canberra, who later turned out to be a KGB agent and was expelled from the country. ASIO monitored Combe's conversations and meetings with Ivanov. It also alleged – wrongly – that Combe's wife had travelled to the Soviet Union at Moscow's expense and that Combe had met one of Prime Minister Hawke's closest advisers, Bob Hogg, while he was under investigation.

As the affair grabbed the headlines, Labor politicians accused ASIO of mounting a campaign designed to smear the ALP. Partly in an attempt to cool down passions that had been aroused by the Combe affair, Hawke asked Justice Hope to conduct a second inquiry into Australia's intelligence agencies. His report was published in 1985.

It generally praised ASIO and found no evidence that the agency had indulged in unlawful activities. However, Hope proposed a package of further measures to ensure not only that ASIO would be kept under permanent scrutiny, partly by strengthening the attorney-general's control over the agency, but also to inspire more public trust and confidence in the organisation.

## *Statutory controls*

Hope's proposals led to the 1986 ASIO Amendment Act and the appointment of an inspector-general (IG) of Security and Intelligence. The Labor Government went beyond Hope's recommendations by also deciding to set up a Joint Parliamentary Committee on Intelligence with members selected from all parties in the Senate and the House of Representatives.

The Committee has seven members – three from the Senate, four from the House of Representatives – selected by party leaders subject to the approval of the Senate and the House as a whole. The Committee's members are not subject to vetting and hearings are held in private. ASIO officers, including the DG, can give evidence, but ministers can issue a certificate preventing them from doing so and the Committee cannot investigate sensitive current issues or operational methods. The Amendment Act states that the Committee's reports must not disclose the identity of an ASIO officer or classified material and detailed information relating to the methods, sources, targets or results of operations the disclosure of which would, or would be likely to, 'prejudice the performance by the Organisation of its functions'. The Committee is required to seek the advice of the attorney-general before publishing reports. The Act exempts the ASIO Committee from the general rule that the Australian Parliament can authorise the publication of any material given to any of its committees.

Two provisions in the new Act are specifically designed to strengthen the attorney-general's control over ASIO. First, the Act makes it clear that the DG is subject to the directions of the attorney-general. At the same time, there are safeguards against political abuse. The DG may insist that a particular direction must be put in writing and the attorney cannot override the opinion of the DG about the nature of ASIO's advice to the government. The attorney can, however, override the opinion of the DG relating to surveillance of an individual, but only by a written direction setting out the attorney's reasons for challenging ASIO's opinion. A copy of the direction has to be sent to the IG.

The attorney-general also has the authority to issue new written guidelines to ASIO's DG. The guidelines have to be tabled in Parliament within 15 days of their issue. Material regarded as sensitive would be withheld from Parliament, though the full text has to be provided to the leader of the opposition and to the IG.

In 1986 the Hawke Government announced it had appointed as the country's first IG Neil McInnes, a former journalist who had joined the civil service just eight years previously, rising to the rank of deputy secretary in the prime minister's department. His task is to ensure that Australia's intelligence and security agencies, including the Australian Secret Intelligence Service (ASIS – the equivalent of MI6) and the Defence Signals Directorate (the equivalent of GCHQ), operate legally and protect civil liberties, including the right to privacy.

Before he took up his post on January 1, 1987, McInnes told this writer: 'intelligence agencies are protected to an extent no one else in society enjoys.' He pointed out that the security agencies were exempt from Australia's Freedom of Information Act and said their activities were not open to proper criticism. 'It is natural in a democracy for these agencies to be subjected to a special form of control,' he said. He made a particular point of mentioning the Defence Signals Department (DSD), Australia's link in the five-nation network which includes GCHQ and America's National Security Agency, acknowledging that there had been allegations that DSD had intercepted private communications.

The IG's job is to ensure that Australia's security and intelligence agencies do not break the law and keep to guidelines laid down by ministers. He or she can investigate the propriety of particular activities and any action which 'may be inconsistent with or contrary to any human right, being an act or practice referred to the inspector-general by the Human Rights Commission'.[36]

The inspector-general can investigate complaints about ASIO's adverse security vetting reports on an individual and investigate whether a minister's decision to ask ASIO to collect and pass on information about an individual is justified on genuine security grounds.

The IG can also conduct investigations at the request of the minister responsible for the different intelligence agencies, or at the request of the prime minister. He or she can investigate a complaint by a member of the public or by an official of the agencies and can also launch an investigation on his or her own initiative. The IG has the power to enter the premises of any intelligence agency. Officials will be fined if they try to prevent this.

## *Terms and targets*

The 1986 Act states that ASIO 'shall not limit the right of persons to engage in lawful advocacy, protest or dissent and the exercise of the right shall not, by itself, be regarded as prejudicial to security, and the functions of the Organisation shall be construed accordingly.'

In response to criticisms made by Justice Hope, the new Act also abandoned the use of the terms 'subversive' and 'terrorism' as being too broad and open to too much subjective interpretation. These terms are replaced by three new classes of activity: 'politically motivated violence (PMV)', 'promotion of communal violence', and 'attacks on Australia's defence system'. The move was welcomed by ASIO in its annual report as assisting 'in setting boundaries for proper involvement in some more sensitive areas of security investigation'.[37]

PMV is defined in the Act as:

> acts or threats of violence or unlawful harm that are intended or likely to achieve a political objective, whether in Australia or elsewhere, including acts or threats carried on for the purpose of influencing the policy or acts of a government, whether in Australia or elsewhere; acts that
> 1) involve violence or are intended or are likely to involve or lead to violence (whether by the persons who carry out those acts or by other persons); and
> 2) are directed to overthrowing or destroying, or assisting in the overthrow or destruction of, the government or the constitutional system of government of the Commonwealth (of Australia) or of a State or Territory.

ASIO's definition of PMV also refers to laws covering crimes, including hijacking.[38]

The new legislation extends the existing controls over warrants issued for telephone-taps to new 'listening devices' and new types of bugs. It allows ASIO to collect 'foreign intelligence' in Australia – i.e. relating to the intentions or activities of foreign powers – but adds a proviso preventing the director-general from requesting a warrant under this heading to collect information relating to an Australian citizen or company. The Act also requires records of tapped conversations to be destroyed if they are not directly relevant to ASIO's functions.

## Conclusion

Britain has a special intelligence relationship with its three most trusted allies who swap information under the terms of the secret UKUSA Treaty signed shortly after the second world war – the US, Canada and Australia. Over the past decade, governments in these countries – Liberal, Conservative, Labour, Republican or Democrat – have introduced reforms to make their security services increasingly accountable to an independent body or to parliamentary or Congressional committees. They have recognised the need for oversight because of the exceptional role, influence and power of these agencies. In some cases, notably in the US, reforms were effectively forced on governments. In other cases, governments have come round to the view that more openness and accountability are beneficial – helping to promote both trust and efficiency.

We can learn from the experience of these countries. There is a need, as the US Congress has demonstrated, for legislative oversight committees to be backed up by adequate staff. Both Canada and Australia have inspector generals independent of both government and the oversight committees but who help those committees. Canada, for the present, has avoided what we believe to be an essential feature of any oversight system – a parliamentary committee – although its independent Review Committee has wide powers, including the right to see any papers of the country's security and intelligence agency. The view in Canada was that a parliamentary oversight committee would get distracted by partisan feuds and would make the system vulnerable to leaks. US experience, however, has shown that elected representatives can keep genuine secrets and that it is governments and infighting government agencies who are responsible for the vast majority of leaks of sensitive information. We believe that in a democracy, it is to democratic representatives that security and intelligence agencies – who supposedly operate in our name – should be held to account.

The US, Australia and Canada have, to varying degrees, recognised the grey area, dangerous in any democracy, between dissent and genuine threats to democratic institutions and national security. Thus in Australia the term 'subversion' has been abandoned and in Canada, the Counter-Subversion Branch of the security service has been abolished. These countries have had their share of scandals, with security officials overstepping the mark.

But so, too, has Britain. MI5 has indulged in illegal activities and broken its own guidelines. Disclosures in the US that the CIA had indulged in similar practices – infiltrating domestic groups, targeting individuals for political reasons – provoked outrage. In Britain, only a small group has protested. In 1967 the British press revealed that all private cables and telexes leaving Britain were made available to the intelligence services. Nothing happened. When similar practices were revealed in the US in 1975, it led to stricter controls, including legislation.

What is the explanation for the different reaction? The answer, according to the former CIA Director, Stansfield Turner, is what he calls 'the much more deeply ingrained attitude in Britain about the necessity for secrecy in intelligence.' The British public, he says, is willing to accept greater intrusions into its privacy and more limitations on what it can know about intelligence activities.[39]

The difference in attitude and approach, therefore, can be summed up in two words: misplaced deference.

# CHAPTER EIGHT

# The Case for Accountability

'Whilst the Security Service remains a totally independent and unaccountable body, public suspicion will continue to grow, and in turn secrecy will become more obsessive.' So wrote Miranda Ingram shortly after her former colleague, Michael Bettaney, was sentenced to 23 years in prison for trying to pass secrets to the Russians.[1] 'You are trained', she stated a year later, 'to be suspicious, to assume the worst motive in the simplest of actions – it is the very nature of the work.'[2]

## A distorted view?

Insiders suggest that secrecy and lack of accountability have prevented the security services from having a balanced view of the real world. The former Minister of Defence official, Clive Ponting, found senior MI5 officers far to the right: 'They're utterly reactionary, tucked away in their little world of their own.'[3]

The journalist Chapman Pincher has described a conversation he had with Harold Macmillan. The former Conservative Prime Minister, according to Pincher, said that 'the secret world was so peculiar that anyone who spent more than 10 years in it was likely to be weird and even mad.'[4]

The former CIA director, Stansfield Turner, has argued that oversight helped the CIA to keep in touch with public opinion and the national mood. 'It is particularly easy', he commented, 'to become isolated in a profession as secretive as intelligence.'[5] Peter Wright's *Spycatcher* shows what damage can be done by those living in a fevered world feeding on suspicion and bureaucratic jealousies. Former MI5 officer Cathy Massiter has spoken of the 'hothouse' relationship between MI5 and the rest of Whitehall: 'It was a kind of looking over the shoulder, a fear of being caught out, a fear of not being seen to be doing enough, and therefore open to criticism.'[6]

We have seen how the Canadian Security Intelligence Service fought against pressure to rely more on open sources. The Franks Committee of Privy Councillors set up to investigate the events leading up to the Argentine invasion of the Falklands in 1982 pointed to a similar failing in British intelligence. But it was one mistake among many highlighted in its Falkland Islands Review published in January 1983.[7]

The Franks Committee showed how, during the months before the invasion, the Joint Intelligence Organisation in the Cabinet Office repeatedly confirmed its own assumption that an invasion was highly unlikely. The Latin America

Current Intelligence Group (CIG) of the Joint Intelligence Organisation met 18 times between July 1981 and March 1982 (when the Argentines invaded), yet not once did it discuss the Falklands. The Committee also spelt out how the JIO was either unaware of, or misinterpreted, the Argentine press campaign against British sovereignty of the Islands in the beginning of 1982. The Committee said:

> As a result it seems to us that [the assessments staff] may have attached greater significance to the secret intelligence, which at that time was reassuring about the prospects of an early move to confrontation... The changes in the Argentine position were, we believe, more evident on the diplomatic front and in the associated press campaign than in the intelligence reports.[8]

While the intelligence agencies can be blind to political realities and developments, they can also exaggerate insignificant ones to suit their prejudices. Equally, governments can be tempted to rely either too much on the agencies or too little, depending on their prejudices. At other times, security and intelligence services can doctor their reports and assessments simply to please their political masters. These dangers are all the greater when the public may assume, given all the sophisticated intelligence-gathering methods at their disposal, that the government – unlike the rest of us – really does know what is going on. Secrecy and lack of independent oversight compound these problems and temptations.

## Arguments against accountability

The Thatcher Government – in common with its predecessors – insists that the security and intelligence services must be shielded by total secrecy if they are to function effectively. It rejects any system of outside, independent, scrutiny on the grounds that outsiders – whether MPs, privy councillors or judges – could never be in a position to make a judgment about the rights and wrongs of why and how the security services acted as they did in any particular case.

Time and again during the passage through Parliament of the Security Service Act, government ministers argued that an independent body which was allowed inside what they called the 'barrier of secrecy' would have no effective function – and would simply encourage false expectations – since it would not be able to disclose anything it had learned there to anyone outside that barrier, including MPs. And if the body itself was outside the barrier, it would not have access to the necessary material to carry out its task and would thus be equally unconvincing.

The clear message behind this argument against a parliamentary oversight committee is that MPs, including those who are privy councillors, cannot be trusted with information about the activities of the security services: they would leak sensitive information, they would not understand its significance, or they would use it to score partisan points.

The Government insisted during the parliamentary debates on the Security Service Act that any independent scrutiny would dilute, or muddle, the responsibility of the prime minister and the home secretary to the Commons. The Government sticks rigidly to the formal constitutional convention that ministers, and *only* ministers, are responsible to Parliament for the activities of the executive – including the security services.

It has been argued that the separation of powers under the American constitution – with the executive consisting of an unelected cabinet and a president who are not members of the legislature – makes a system of legislative oversight more necessary in the US. In Britain, the argument goes, ministers, all of them MPs, are answerable to Parliament. But this ignores the decision by other Commonwealth countries, with constitutions modelled on the Westminster system, to introduce a system of independent or parliamentary oversight of their security services. It also ignores the refusal of ministers here to answer any questions about the security and intelligence agencies.

The Government – both its ministers and senior civil servants – also argues that a Watergate or Irangate could not happen in Britain. This argument is based on the assumption that the British system is not so open to corruption or misconduct as the American and that ministers do not mislead Parliament. Sir Robert Armstrong, the then Cabinet Secretary, asserted that a Watergate could not happen here when he was questioned by MPs about the Westland affair – specifically, about the leaking of part of a letter from the Solicitor-General in 1986. The role of the Prime Minister and her own close advisers in the affair has still not been explained.

The Government argues that ministers must be given a free hand. It dismissed an amendment to the Security Service Act whereby decisions of the proposed Security Service Commissioner – a senior judge – could be open to appeal in the courts on the grounds that it would undermine and 'usurp' the responsibility of ministers.[9] And, the Government argues, it would not be right for warrants to be issued only on a judge's authority even though this is the practice in the US, Canada and Australia.

A proposal whereby an annual report to Parliament by the prime minister would give an account of MI5 opinion on current threats and priorities – the practice in the US, Italy and West Germany – was described by John Patten as 'unreasonable and unsafe'.[10]

Pressed to explain why Britain alone among western democracies could not adopt a system of independent oversight to which its security and intelligence agencies should be called to account, the Government argues that Britain is in a unique position. Britain, Whitehall says, is faced with unique problems and unique threats – an apparent reference to Northern Ireland. (Ministers are also quick to claim that their counterparts in those countries with a system of accountability are envious of the absence of independent scrutiny in Britain.)

Another, perhaps more profound, argument employed against giving Parliament any role in scrutinising the activities of the security services is that Parliament could never sanction those activities. The former Lord Chancellor, Lord Hailsham, was asked in the BBC Radio 4 series, 'My Country Right or Wrong', whether he thought a parliamentary committee should be set up to oversee the security services. He replied: 'I don't think it can be done because the security services, I'm sure ... are by common accounts commonly doing things which can't be justified in law. And, that being so, Parliament could never approve it, nor could any organisation employed by Parliament possibly countenance it.'[11] Hailsham was asked the question in response to Lord Donaldson, Master of the Rolls, (the Senior Appeal Court judge), who made remarks to the effect that the security services could not be expected to follow the strict letter of the law. It was a matter of 'common sense', he said during the *Spycatcher* trial.

The Security Service Act, which puts MI5 on a statutory footing, has introduced a curious conundrum. The Act was passed by Parliament. But all Parliament has really done is to transfer to statutory legislation the powers that were previously given under Crown prerogative. The Act has legalised secret bugging and burglary – activities that would be illegal if carried out by anyone else – and given parliamentary blessing to the absolute, personal, discretion of the home secretary. It has made lawful what was previously unlawful.

## Arguments for accountability

No part of the executive, or area of activity by agents of the state, should be immune from parliamentary scrutiny. No government agency should spend taxpayers' money without parliamentary approval. For centuries these have been regarded as fundamental constitutional principles. Successive governments have paid lip-service to these principles, but have always claimed an exception for the security and intelligence services.

This may seem an acceptable argument until, that is, we consider the past record of the security services and the extent of their power and influence.

The allies with whom Britain most closely co-operates all have a system of independent oversight precisely because they recognise the dangers of abuse. 'It is not good enough', the former CIA Director, Stansfield Turner, has said, 'for intelligence agencies to be accountable to the executive.' There is a need, he says in his book, *Democracy and Secrecy*, 'for a responsible body outside the executive branch to make sure that the executive is not over-enthusiastic in seeking to obtain information important to the national interest. Over-enthusiasm, as we have seen, may lead to excess.'[12]

The point has been underlined by Harvey Barnett, recently retired head of ASIO, Australia's equivalent of MI5. 'The Security Service', he says in his autobiography, *Tale of the Scorpion*, 'should, and can, expect clear guidance from Parliament' about what activities it may carry out and what methods may be used.[13] This is especially important, he argues, since security services may, in aiming at the overall good of the community, be required to infringe temporarily on certain aspects of individual liberty. 'It would be a sign of political health and common-sense', Barnett adds, 'to have at least occasional external scrutiny of a body which may be required for national purposes to intrude into the private lives of individuals.'[14]

Barnett opposed the Australian Labor Government's decision to set up a parliamentary committee on ASIO. Nevertheless, he acknowledged that one positive feature of this initiative was that MPs serving on it would have the opportunity 'to learn something of the difficulties, the successes and the hard work which are part of ASIO's daily life'.

## *Public confidence*

This points to another argument in favour of the accountability of the security and intelligence services: accountability and openness can promote public trust and mutual understanding. 'Oversight', Turner noted, 'was helpful in restoring the CIA's public image. If the CIA was attacked in the press, the Congressional committees standing up for us naturally carried more credibility with the public than anything we could say in our own defence. Once the committees had learned enough about intelligence to understand what we were doing and why, they were indeed willing to support us.'[15]

The Anglo-American Ditchley Foundation – a body which, as we have seen, organises periodic conferences for the 'great and the good' – invited public figures to a weekend at its country house near Oxford in October 1988. The general conclusion of the country weekend, according to those who attended, was that the British Government's blanket cloak of secrecy over the activities of the security and intelligence services – what they described as the 'absurdity factor' – tended to undermine public confidence both in government and in the services the government sought to protect, damaged morale in those services and possibly led to lower levels of support for adequate funding. Simon Jenkins, then a *Sunday Times* columnist and now editor of *The Times*, who participated, wrote 'a personal essay' about the conference. He said he had not before attended a Ditchley conference at which the Americans had been able to say so emphatically to the British: 'We have seen the future and it is not as awful as you think.'[16]

Even the most sceptical Americans at the conference, Jenkins reported, accepted that the advantages of independent accountability outweighed the disadvantages. No covert operation was believed to have been compromised by oversight. The intelligence community had recovered a reputation tarnished by Watergate. Morale, recruitment and status had improved and resources were easier to come by. Oversight had made intelligence 'less self-serving and more useful to policy-makers, better managed and more sophisticated.' Jenkins concluded that most participants felt that Britain could not go on ignoring the arguments for independent, democratic, oversight of its security and intelligence services for ever.[17]

The British Government suggests that it is those in the so-called 'fevered and partisan' world of Westminster who cannot be trusted. It implies that MPs would be quick to leak sensitive information they were given about the security services. Evidence from those countries with a system of parliamentary and independent oversight does not bear this out. Turner says he found the US Congress Intelligence Committees 'as responsible as any sector of government, especially when it came to protecting our sources'.[18] A Senator or Congressman suspected of leaking details of operations would immediately be reported to the Congress Ethics Committee and this could devastate his or her political career.

The evidence anyway suggests that far from preventing them, secrecy and lack of accountability actually promote leaks. MI5, observed Mr Justice Powell, the Sydney judge who so roundly dismissed the Government's attempt to ban *Spycatcher* in Australia, had been leaking 'like a sieve'.[19] He was referring to the series of books about the security services, notably by the authors Chapman Pincher and Niger West. Despite the absolute ban on disclosures by members or former members of the security and intelligence services (enshrined in the Government's new Official Secrets Act), they will continue to leak information in their own interest and to those writers whom they favour. Official leaks and disinformation are protected by official secrecy.

## *Sophisticated technology*

The need for accountability becomes even more essential as intelligence agencies, as well as military commanders, allow themselves to be at the mercy of increasingly sophisticated technology. It is becoming more difficult for a CIA officer at his desk or a GCHQ analyst in Cheltenham, let alone a commander on action stations, to interpret the information which sophisticated technology provides. The wood cannot be seen for the trees, the real danger cannot be identified, as the raw data pours in.

Thus, for example, both the CIA and British intelligence, bombarded with information about political upheavals around the world, were heavily criticised for failing to foresee the overthrow of the Shah. The US intelligence community failed to predict the 1975 Middle East war. Spy satellites may help to verify whether arms control agreements are being honoured and provide such detailed information (as former President Carter once boasted) that Washington could identify individual cars entering the compound of the US embassy in Teheran during the hostage crisis in 1980. But most crises, however they start, are ended by human judgment. Those judgments should not be made by humans who have a monopoly of information, who know they need not share their knowledge, and who have power without responsibility.

## *Power and influence*

Security and intelligence agencies must be held to account to ensure that ministers are themselves in control of the instruments at their command; at present the agencies are not properly accountable even to ministers, let alone to Parliament. They must be held to account to ensure that they are efficient and not a waste of public money – secrecy encourages inefficiency. They must be accountable for the simple reason that they have widespread power over ordinary citizens. Their power and influence ranges from the exotic – the management (or manipulation) of international crises – to the mundane – the vetting and surveillance of ordinary men and women.

Their role, by definition, involves the use of covert means to intrude upon individual freedoms and privacy. They have unique access to information which they hold on millions of records, the contents of which are secret and frequently misleading or inaccurate. They hold information not only on those whom they regard as genuine threats to 'national security', but also on individual citizens simply because of their political beliefs.

It is not a question of the security services accounting for every administrative decision and operation or exercising discretion before they can act. It should be the role of the courts to examine warrants for intercepting communications, for example, or entering premises. Parliamentary oversight should concentrate on monitoring activities and examining priorities. But a parliamentary committee would need to have access to information it asks for – and be given sound reasons if it is not being provided with it – before Parliament, and the public, may say they are in any position to trust the security services.

## Conclusion

It is an uncomfortable reality that for the foreseeable future democracies are going to have security and intelligence services, if only to safeguard the democratic system and their citizens against physical attacks including violence – notably terrorism – rooted in political or ideological causes.

To carry out this significant, but specific, task, agencies have to gather (accurate) intelligence in advance of possible outrages. In the face of it, this seems uncontroversial. But experience has shown that without a robust system of independent oversight, the system is wide open to abuse. Security services are unable to resist the temptation to indulge in activities that have no place in a democracy. The cure can be as dangerous as the disease.

The activities of Britain's security and intelligence apparatus strike at the heart of civil liberties, the right to privacy (which, in Britain, remains little more than a shibboleth), and the relationship between Parliament, the citizen and the executive.

By tradition, it is up to Parliament to reign in an over mighty executive and for the courts, applying the principles of common law, to strike a balance between conflicting interests. Under the Security Service Act, Parliament will have no more say in the scrutiny of MI5 than it had before - that is, none at all. The courts will have no role and the Act specifically says that the decisions of the Security Service Commissioner and the complaints tribunal will not be open to challenge in the courts. During the recent *Spycatcher* litigation, the Government argued that the courts had no role in adjudicating disputes about the disclosure of information concerning the security and intelligence agencies. This claim prompted Mr Justice Scott in his High Court ruling to remark:

> No question of a balance between the proper requirements of national security, on the one hand, and of freedom of speech or of the press, on the other hand, arose. I found myself unable to escape the reflection that the absolute protection of the security services that Sir Robert (Armstrong, then the Cabinet Secretary and the Government's chief witness) was contending for could not be achieved this side of the Iron Curtain.[20]

This observation is even more pertinent as that curtain drops.

The first page of the Rockefeller report commissioned by President Ford after Watergate, and the other scandals involving US agencies, said that while it was vital that security requirements be met it was equally important that intelligence activities should be conducted without impairing our democratic institutions and fundamental freedoms.

Twenty years earlier when the Government appeared to take a more relaxed approach about former members of the security and intelligence services writing their memoirs (even at the height of the Cold War), Sir Percy Sillitoe, the former head of the Security Service, wrote about the dangers of a police state:

> I myself, at any rate, would rather see two or three traitors slip through the net of the Security Service than be a party to the taking of measures which would be calculated to result in such a regime.[21]

The Government says 'trust us' to ensure the security and intelligence agencies do not abuse their power and their uniquely privileged status. The former Home Secretary Douglas Hurd has made it clear that the Government does not trust MPs, even a committee of privy councillors, to oversee their activities. It has not explained why Britain is so different from other countries, including Canada, Australia, and the United States which have a system of parliamentary or independent oversight. The Government wants to avoid a proper debate on the important issue of the role of a security service in a mature democracy. The timing of the Security Service Act and the haste with which it was pushed through Parliament prompt the suspicion that ministers wanted to draw the teeth from critics of its new Official Secrets Act with its blanket ban on disclosures by members of the security and intelligence services. The MI5 Act was dictated by political, tactical and presentational considerations. It was not prompted by a serious desire to confront the problem.

Other western countries have done so, first by laying down a set of fundamental principles guiding the operations of the security and intelligence services and secondly by developing a framework for holding them to account. The Security Service Act dismisses the problem in just two paragraphs. In Canada, a Royal Commission recently devoted two volumes and 1,200 pages to *Freedom and Security Under the Law*. It started with the premise that there are a number of 'essential requirements' of a democracy: responsible government, the rule of law and freedom of legitimate political dissent. As requirements, it insisted, they are 'not to be compromised, whittled down or balanced off to make effective security possible'. Special laws may be needed for security and intelligence agencies but it is not for the agencies to pick and choose when the law applies to them. If members of the agencies break the law, then they must be brought to justice like anyone else.

The five basic principles laid down by the McDonald Commission to govern the Canadian Security Intelligence Service (CSIS) can surely be applied with equal strength to Britain's security and intelligence agencies (see below). The balance to be struck is crucial, since by definition security and intelligence services secretly interfere with the individual's privacy without the individual knowing the case against them. The issues are so fundamental, the temptation to overstep the mark so great, that it is not for ministers to say 'leave it all to us'. Parliament, and this, of course, includes members of the opposition parties, must have a monitoring role. There is in Whitehall at present an unhealthy and cynical contempt for Parliament. Perhaps too many MPs have become used to being deprived of information by ministers and civil servants and have become complacent. To acquiesce in this compounds the danger.

## Recommendations

The Government knows its cursory Security Service Act is not the end of the matter. But it hopes the measure, notably the complaints tribunal, represents the minimum it can get away with for the time being, at least to satisfy the European Court of Human Rights. As we have seen, the Court has twice, in cases involving West Germany and Sweden, ruled that governments must provide 'adequate and effective safeguards against abuse' of the powers of the security services.[22] It is doubtful, however, whether the Security Service Act satisfies Article 8 of the European Human Rights Convention, which covers the right to privacy and Article 13 which says that an effective remedy must exist in domestic law.

Whether the Strasbourg Court considers that the Government's Security Service Act goes far enough has not yet been fully tested. Certainly, the complaints procedures do not extend as far as those adopted by other countries: for example, decisions of the complaints tribunal and the Security Service Commissioner are not subject to appeal in the courts. The tribunal and the commissioner will investigate privately and report in private to the home secretary. Individuals will not necessarily have any way of knowing whether they have been subjected to bugging or burglary or vetting by MI5, whether authorised or not. Similarly, the tribunal set up by the 1985 Interception of Communications Act, which was also introduced after pressure from the European Court of Human Rights, is under no obligation to inform individuals either that their telephone has been tapped with a properly authorised warrant or that the proper procedures were not followed. The tribunal also has no way of knowing whether the Security Service has employed private detective agencies to tap phones.

Furthermore, the Government's Security Service Act is not even an adequate starting point. Parliament should seize the opportunity to spell out the basic principles which must guide the Security Service, Special Branch and Britain's two other main intelligence agencies – MI6 and GCHQ. Learning from the experience of other Commonwealth countries, machinery should be set up for an acceptable form of parliamentary scrutiny of *all* of Britain's security and intelligence agencies.

- Following the Canadian model, the basic principles governing the activities of all the security and intelligence services should be:

  1. The rule of law is paramount.
  2. The means of investigation must be proportional to the gravity of the threat.
  3. The need for investigative techniques must be weighed against the damage they might do to personal freedom and privacy.
  4. The more intrusive the technique, the higher the authority required to approve its use.
  5. Except in emergencies, less intrusive techniques must be preferred to more intrusive ones.

Accounts from former security and intelligence officers suggest that on occasion the State indulges in the same practices and adopts the same cavalier attitude to democratic rights as those from whom the State is supposed to protect us. The function of all security and intelligence services should be the protection of the security of Britain against threats from violence and espionage, including terrorism.

- Parliament should follow the example set by Australia and Canada and abandon the concept of *'subversion'*, however it is dressed up. The same applies to the term 'national security'. They are both too loose, too subjective and too open-ended and should be replaced by a statutorily defined term which should be limited to the following ingredients: unlawful and/or violent acts intended to destroy or overthrow the constitutionally established system of government. The emphasis must be on *unlawful* or *violent* activities including espionage and sabotage. The right to lawful advocacy, protest or dissent should be explicitly protected.

- The security and intelligence services should collect, analyse and retain certain information only to the extent defined as *'strictly necessary'* by Parliament and the courts and should do so in a covert way only when all other means, and open sources, have been tried and failed. The Data Protection Registrar should have an independent watchdog role to ensure that the information held by the security and intelligence services complies with the Data Protection principles.

- The Security Service and the Special Branch (both when it is acting on behalf of MI5 or in its own security and intelligence role), should be *accountable to Parliament* – and not, as at present, merely to the Home Secretary. The anomaly whereby GCHQ and MI6 are excluded from any statutory recognition should be remedied and they, too, should be monitored by Parliament.

- *Directors General* of the Security Service, of the Secret Intelligence Service and of GCHQ (DGs) should be appointed by the government after consultation with leaders of all parties represented in Parliament and a Commons select committee on security and intelligence (see below). As in Canada they should be appointed initially for a period of five years, but could be reappointed for a second period of five years with a maximum of ten years. They would present an annual report to Parliament.

- The Commons committee, after consultation with the leaders of all parties represented in Parliament, would appoint an *Inspector General* (IG) of the security and intelligence services. The IG would have the right of access to all information, including files on individuals, in the hands of the security and intelligence agencies. He or she would also review the DG's annual reports to Parliament. The IG would function as a back-up to the Commons committee, helping to ensure that the security and intelligence services are keeping to their existing guidelines.

- *A parliamentary select committee on security and intelligence* should be set up with about 20 members reflecting the overall party balance in the Commons. This is the most democratic and accountable of all the possible models. The members of the committee would be appointed by their respective parties. The committee would be supported by adequate research and secretarial staff. It would have the final say over the total budgets of the security and intelligence services and scrutinise how the money is spent. It would hold regular hearings, private where necessary, and have the power to subpoena witnesses and make recommendations. It would periodically draw up written guidelines covering the activities of the security and intelligence services.

- The committee, like the IG, would have access to all information held by the agencies, with the possible exception of information relating to current or imminent operations. The committee would initially receive the information on a confidential basis. However, it would draw up an *annual report* based on its scrutiny and investigations for Parliament. It would consult with the IG and the heads of the different agencies about which, if any, parts of the report should remain confidential but the final decision as to which information should be published, and which kept secret, would be up to the committee. The committee would also be provided with any reports or recommendations of the IG including details about the number of warrants for telephone-tapping, bugging and house entering, the reasons for them and the targets affected. The committee could ask the IG to help with its investigations.

- The DGs would have to *apply for warrants* for telephone-tapping, burglaries and bugging to a *High Court judge*. The application would have to be accompanied by an affidavit setting out in detail why they were needed, how other investigative techniques had failed or would be unlikely to succeed, the object of the warrants and the people or group targeted. The judge would be able to impose conditions on the use of a warrant, as well as the use to which the information gained as a result of the operation would be put and for how long records of the information were to be kept. A warrant would be valid for no more than one month initially, though it would be renewable under the same conditions. At the end of any operation the IG should ensure that the target was informed of what had taken place other than when this would be prejudicial to necessary ongoing security operations.

- Complaints from the public about the activities of the security and intelligence agencies would be heard by an *independent tribunal* consisting of the IG sitting with two assessors. Complaints would relate to any actions of the security services against individuals or against organisations. They could also relate to house entering or interception of communications as well as employment vetting – secret negative vetting would no longer take place – and the denial of visas. The complainant would be allowed a legal representative at the hearings. S/he would be informed by the tribunal of the decisions made following its investigation and the reasons for them. Complainants would have the right to appeal to the courts if they were dissatisfied with the conclusions of the tribunal and could bring a civil action against the agency involved. Members of the security and intelligence services with evidence of malpractice within the services could also take their complaints to the tribunal.

- The *Official Secrets Act* should be *repealed* and *replaced* by a *Freedom of Information Act* along the lines of US legislation. There would be limited exceptions, governed by clearly defined criteria, to the general rule that all information should be publicly available. The onus would be on the government to show why any information it claims is sensitive should be withheld. The government's decisions would be open to appeal to the Courts. Section 1 of the 1911 Official Secrets Act would be retained as an express Espionage Act.

- The *Data Protection Act* would be *amended* to give individuals *the right to see all records* held on them – both on computer and manual files – by all government agencies. A refusal to do so, including a refusal by any of the security and intelligence services – on 'national security' grounds, for example – could be challenged on appeal to the courts.

- The *Interception of Communications Act* would be *amended* to cover all means of tapping through new technology.

- The *Public Record Act* would also be *amended*, abandoning the present wide measure of discretion which allows government departments and agencies to withhold archives from public view. A parliamentary committee, independent of Whitehall, would monitor the way records are disclosed and withheld from public view.

- The use of *private security firms* by the security and intelligence services would be *outlawed*.

Central to any government in a real democracy is an effective system of checks and balances. That, we are told, is one of the pillars of Britain's unwritten constitution. Ministers, we are also told, are accountable to Parliament for their actions and for those of all their officials.

This is palpably untrue – if only on a practical level. It is *demonstrably* untrue when it comes to the activities of the security and intelligence services – agencies which have a unique, secret power to interfere in people's privacy, wreck careers and undermine civil liberties. These agencies can be the sleeping engines of authoritarianism behind the daily practices of parliamentary democracy. In a period when demands for accountable security services are beginning to have an effect in Eastern Europe, is it not time for the British Government to open our security services to effective democratic scrutiny?

# APPENDIX I

## A Summary of the Main Provisions of the Official Secrets Act 1989

The 1989 Official Secrets Act repeals the 'catch-all' Section 2 of the 1911 Official Secrets Act. Section 1 of the 1911 Act, which deals with espionage, is retained. (The 1920 and 1939 Acts are also still in force.)

Under Section 1 of the 1989 Act, a member or former member of the security and intelligence services 'is guilty of an offence if without lawful authority he discloses any information, document, or other article relating to security and intelligence which is or has been in his possession by virtue of his position as a member of any of those services.'

Also covered by this blanket ban is 1) any statement by existing or former members of the security and intelligence service which 'purports' to be information relating to those services, and 2) any official who has been notified that he or she will be treated as though they were members of the security and intelligence services.

Section 1 says that 'security and intelligence' means 'the work of, or in support of, the security and intelligence services or any part of them', and references to information relating to security or intelligence include 'references to information held or transmitted by those services or by persons in support of, or any part of, them.'

Section 2 states that anyone who is or has been a Crown servant or government contractor is guilty of an offence if without lawful authority he makes 'a damaging disclosure' of any information or document relating to defence. A disclosure is damaging, it says, if it damages the capability of any part of the armed forces of the Crown to carry out their tasks or leads to loss of life or injury to members of those forces or serious damage to the equipment or installations of those forces or 'endangers the interests of the United Kingdom abroad, seriously obstructs the promotion or protection by the United Kingdom of those interests or endangers the safety of British citizens abroad', or 'it is of information or of a document or article which is such that its unauthorised disclosure would be likely to have any of those effects.'

'Defence', it states, means:

(a) the size, shape, organisation, logistics, order of battle, deployment, operations, state of readiness and training of the armed forces of the Crown;

(b) the weapons, stores or other equipment of those forces and the invention, development, production and operation of such equipment and research relating to it;
(c) defence policy and strategy and military planning and intelligence;
(d) plans and measures for the maintenance of essential supplies and services that are or would be needed in times of war.

Section 3 deals with international relations. Officials and former officials, or government contractors are guilty of any offence if they make a damaging disclosure of:
(a) any information, document or other article relating to international relations; or
(b) any confidential information, document or other article which was obtained from a state other than the United Kingdom or an international organisation.

A disclosure is damaging, it says, if:
(a) it endangers the interests of the United Kingdom abroad, seriously obstructs the promotion or protection by the United Kingdom of those interests or endangers the safety of British citizens abroad; or
(b) it is of information or of a document or article which is such that its unauthorised disclosure would be likely to have any of those effects.'

'The fact that [the information] is confidential, or its nature or contents', the Act says, 'may be sufficient to establish that the information, document r articme would likely to be damaging.'

Section 4 covers disclosures on which an absolute ban is applied to third parties – journalists, for instance – as well as existing or former members of the security and intelligence services. It deals with 'crime and special investigation powers' (the latter phrase is a reference to the activities of the security services). It is a blanket ban on disclosing information which 'results in the commission of an offence', or 'facilitates an escape from legal cuqtody', r 'impedes the prevention or detection of offences', or would be likely to have such effects.

This section also applies to any information relating to, and obtained from, telephone tapping under the 1985 Interception of Communications Act, or to surveillance and property-entering by MI5 covered by the 1989 Security Service Act.

Section 5 relates to third parties, such as journalists, who receive information relating to the categories covered by earlier sections. But there is no absolute ban – editors, writers, and others receiving information from officials without authority would be guilty if their disclosures were 'damaging' or if they had reasonable cause to believe they were.

Section 5 also applies the criteria of earlier sections to disclosure by a third party of information sent by the British government to foreign states or international organisations.

Under Section 8, it is an offence to refuse 'an official direction' for the return of a document disclosed without 'lawful authority'.

Section 9 states that all prosecutions under the Act must have the consent of the Attorney-General.

# APPENDIX II

## A Summary of the Main Provisions of the Security Services Act 1989

Section 1 of the Act places the Security Service 'under the authority of the Secretary of State'. MI5's functions, it says, shall be 'the protection of national security and, in particular, its protection against threats from espionage, terrorism and sabotage, from the activities of agents of foreign powers *and from actions intended to overthrow or undermine parliamentary democracy by political, industrial or violent means.*' (Our emphasis – this phrase is the Government's official definition of subversion.)

Amendments which had the backing of backbenchers of all parties in both the Commons and the Lords, which would have confirmed the right of legitimate dissent and excluded lawful protest from MI5's attentions, were dismissed by the Government on the grounds that this was unnecessary. Home Office ministers argued that the Act should not restrict the scope of MI5's activities on the grounds that it was impossible to foresee future threats to national security and measures to combat them. The Act, said the then Home Secretary, Douglas Hurd, must not stop MI5 from 'moving into new spheres' if necessary.

Section 1 also says that the functions of MI5 will be 'to safeguard the economic well-being of the United Kingdom' against outside threats. Douglas Hurd suggested that this would have included the activities of oil producers during the 1973/74 oil crisis. It appears to give the green light to bugging international companies, commodity brokers and even currency dealers – though these, as we have seen, are primarily GCHQ's targets.

Section 2 says that it will be the Director-General's duty to ensure that 'there are arrangements for securing that no information is obtained ... *except so far as is necessary for the proper discharge of its functions*' a vague phrase open to wide interpretation (our italics).

It will also be the Director-General's duty to ensure that MI5 'does not take any action to further interests of any political party.' This is a weaker form of words than those in the 1952 Maxwell-Fyfe Directive. What happens, asked Lord Mishcon, Labour's front bench spokesman, if the action is against a political party? He proposed an amendment to add the phrase 'and shall be kept free from any political bias or influence' – a phrase taken from the 1952 Directive. Lord Mackay, the Lord Chancellor, dismissed it. He did so on the grounds that if this additional phrase – even though one which had been included in a charter which was supposed to have governed MI5's activities for the past 37 years – was inserted into the new Act there would be a risk that 'some important activities of the Security Service...would be inhibited or at least would be thought to be inhibited and restricted on the ground that they were political.' This would be the case, Lord Mackay argued, 'notwithstanding that the very political influence that was under question was of a kind which might threaten the security of the United Kingdom as a whole.' Lord Mackay had asked earlier: 'How would the director-general go about the task of keeping every member of the service free from any political influence?'[1]

Section 3 opens with the meat of the Act, wrapped in a double negative. 'No entry on or interference with property', it says, 'shall be unlawful if it is authorised by a warrant issued by the Secretary of State...' It means that bugging and burglary will be legal if it has the official blessing of a senior minister. The former Labour Lord Chancellor, Lord Elwyn-Jones, described the clause as 'breathtaking in its provisions. The issue of a warrant', he noted, 'is to be a purely administrative decision taken by the executive.'[2]

The secretary of state – it could be any secretary of state, the Government has confirmed, though it would usually be the home secretary – can issue a warrant if he 'thinks it necessary' to obtain information which 'is likely to be of substantial value' in assisting MI5 to discharge any of its functions, and if the information 'cannot reasonably be obtained by other means.'

Warrants will be issued initially for a period of six months and will be renewable for a similar period. The secretary of state, the Act says, 'shall cancel a warrant if he is satisfied that the action authorised by it is no longer necessary.' A senior civil servant can issue a warrant 'in an urgent case' provided he or she has the minister's express authority. Warrants issued in this way will usually last for no more than 72 hours except during official holiday periods. Asked why a judge, rather than a minister, should not be responsible for issuing warrants, John Patten, Minister of State at the Home Office, told the Commons that judges might have 'no understanding or experience of security issues'.

Under Section 4, the prime minister appoints a senior judge as a Security Service commissioner. His job is to 'keep under review' the way the secretary of state issues warrants and to send an annual report to the prime minister. His published report would exclude 'any matter [the publication of which] ... would be prejudicial to the continued discharge of the functions of the Service.' Section 4 also states that 'it shall be the duty of every member of the Service and of every official of the department of the secretary of state to disclose or give to the commissioner such documents or information as he may require for the purpose of enabling him to discharge his functions.'

## Complaints procedures under the Act

Section 5 refers to schedules in the Act which spell out the nature of the authority of the commissioner and a tribunal – made up of between three and five lawyers appointed 'by Her Majesty by Royal Warrant' – to investigate complaints about MI5. The Section also states that the decisions of the commissioner and the tribunal 'shall not be subject to appeal or liable to be questioned in any court.' An amendment deleting this ban on appeals to the courts was dismissed by John Patten in the Commons in January 1989 on the grounds that it would 'undermine' the authority of Cabinet Ministers.

The complaints procedures and how they would be followed up – the part of the Act potentially of greatest interest to the general public and which the Government hopes will meet the requirements of the European Convention of Human Rights – are contained in Schedule 1.

'Any person', it begins, 'may complain to the tribunal if he is aggrieved by anything which he believes the Service has done in relation to him or any property of his; and, unless the tribunal consider that the complaint is frivolous or vexatious, they shall investigate it in accordance with the schedule.'

The tribunal will first investigate whether the complainant has been the subject of MI5 'inquiries'. Complaints relating to any 'inquiries' undertaken but finished before the Act came into force will not be investigated. If they had started before then, but were still going on – or, obviously, if they had begun more recently – then the tribunal will determine whether MI5 had 'reasonable grounds' for its actions.

Section 4 of the schedule relates to individuals who are members of groups who are regarded as subversive or threats to national security. If it appears to the tribunal that MI5 instituted inquiries into an individual on the grounds of his or her membership of 'a category of persons' regarded by MI5 as 'requiring investigation', the tribunal shall regard MI5 as having 'reasonable grounds' for deciding to investigate that individual – provided MI5 had 'reasonable grounds' for believing the person to be a member of that group in the first place.

If an individual alleges that MI5 has disclosed information to determine whether he or she should be employed – this is the vetting clause – the tribunal 'shall determine' whether MI5 had 'reasonable grounds' for believing the information to be true.

If the complaint relates to bugging or burglary, the tribunal will refer the matter to the commissioner. He will investigate whether a warrant was issued and whether the secretary of state acted 'properly' in issuing it.

The tribunal essentially deals with complaints relating to information collected by MI5 and its classification of individuals or groups as subversive or national security threats. The commissioner deals with actions – such as bugging or burglary – that require a warrant. If the tribunal concludes that MI5 did not have 'reasonable grounds' for acting, it will tell the complainant and report its findings to the secretary of state and the commissioner. The tribunal will also inform the individual if it, or the commissioner, has not found in his or her favour.

If the tribunal finds in an individual's favour, it 'may' order MI5 investigations to stop and destroy the records and direct the secretary of state to pay compensation. If a complaint about bugging or burglary is upheld, the tribunal 'may...quash [the] warrant.' In such a case, the commissioner can direct the secretary of state to pay compensation.

The tribunal will tell the commissioner if it considers that MI5 was not justified in regarding all members of a particular group or association 'as requiring investigation' by the Security Service. It will also inform the commissioner if in the course of its inquiries it has discovered that MI5 acted 'unreasonably' in another matter. The schedule says that in either of these two cases, the commissioner 'may report' the matter to the secretary of state 'who may take such action in the light of the report *as he thinks fit*' (our emphasis).

In a written parliamentary answer on November 22 1989, the Home Secretary, David Waddington, announced that the Prime Minister had appointed Lord Justice Stuart-Smith, a senior Court of Appeal judge, to be the first Security Service Commissioner. He also announced that the President of the Tribunal was Mr Justice Simon Brown, a High Court judge and former Treasury counsel. Its two other members are Sheriff John McInnes, Sheriff of Tayside Central and Fife, and Sir Richard Gaskell, former President of the Law Society.

# APPENDIX III

# 1984 Home Office Guidelines on the Work of a Special Branch

## Status and organisation

1. Each of the police forces in England and Wales has its own Special Branch. Except for the Metropolitan Police Special Branch, which has responsibilities in relation to Irish Republican extremism and terrorism throughout Great Britain, the responsibility of each Special Branch relates only to the area of the force of which it is a part.

2. All members of a Special Branch are responsible to the chief officer of the force through the head of the Branch and any intervening supervisory ranks in the force structure.

## Specific functions

3. The specific functions listed below comprise those tasks which will most commonly fall to be undertaken by the force Special Branch. However, in some force areas, it may be necessary or desirable for some of these functions to be undertaken by other parts of the force CID or a specialist unit. It will be an operational matter for each chief officer to decide how best to utilise his resources within the force Special Branch.

4. The work of a Special Branch arises from the chief officer's responsibility for *the preservation of the Queen's Peace*. Its work is to assist the chief officer in discharging this responsibility.

5. A Special Branch gathers information about threats to *public order*. Such information will enable the Branch to provide assessments of whether marches, meetings, demonstrations and pickets pose any threat to public order and help the chief officer to determine an appropriate level of policing.

6. A Special Branch assists the Security Service in carrying out its tasks of defending the realm against attempts at espionage and sabotage or from the actions of persons and organisations whether directed from within or without the country which may be judged to be subversive to the State. A large part of this effort is devoted to the study and investigation of terrorism, including the activities of international terrorists and terrorist organisations.

7. A Special Branch provides information about extremists and terrorist groups to the Security Service (or, in the case of Irish Republican extremists and terrorist groups, to the Metropolitan Police Special Branch).

8. A Special Branch assists in the application of the *Travel Notification Scheme* for diplomats and officials.

9. Special Branch officers may provide armed *personal protection* for certain people who are judged to be at risk. Particular attention should be paid to anyone who may plan to harm prominent individuals for political reasons or because of mental disturbance.

10. At airports and seaports, Special Branch officers

- arrest wanted criminals
- detect offences
- gather information relating to their other functions and other criminal matters
- act as examining officers under the legislation on the prevention of terrorism

11. On behalf of the Immigration and Nationality Department of the Home Office, a Special Branch may be asked to carry out naturalisation enquiries, and may assist with immigration enquiries as well as deal with the registration of foreign nationals. A Special Branch may also be involved in prosecutions related to these matters. In practice much of the routine work in these areas may be undertaken by other parts of the force; the appropriate organisational structure will be determined by the size of the force and the number and nature of these enquiries.

12. A Special Branch should enquire into the implications of any offence connected with firearms and explosives unless it is immediately clear that there is no security interest. It may be advisable to include in force orders an instruction that Special Branch be informed immediately of all such cases coming to the notice of the police.

## Relations with others

13. The Metropolitan Police Special Branch is responsible for the assessment of intelligence about Irish Republican extremism and terrorism in Great Britain. Each Special Branch, under the direction of its chief officer, helps the

Metropolitan Police Special Branch in discharging this function.

14. The Metropolitan Police has certain national responsibilities for the provision of personal protection to members of the Royal Family, ministers of the Crown, former ministers, diplomats and other people at risk. Where a Special Branch has protection duties which are connected with the matters which are the responsibility of the Metropolitan Police, the local Special Branch and Metropolitan Police Special Branch or Royalty and Diplomatic Protection Department work in close liaison with each other.

15. The National Joint Unit at New Scotland Yard, which is staffed by officers from Metropolitan and provincial Special Branches, co-ordinates enquiries and applications from police forces in Great Britain concerning people held under prevention of terrorism legislation. The Unit processes, for onward transmission to the Home Office or the Scottish Home and Health Department as the case may be, applications for extension of detention and exclusion orders under the legislation and co-ordinates the preparation of up-to-date assessments in connection with the review of exclusion cases. The National Ports Office, based at Heathrow Airport, provides a liaison and advisory service for ports units in other force areas.

## Records

16. Records should be maintained in order to discharge effectively the functions listed in paragraphs 3-12 above. It is important, however, because of the particular sensitivity of the information concerned, that only information relevant to those functions should be recorded. Close attention should therefore be paid to paragraphs 3-12, and to the definitions given in paragraph 20, in deciding what information should be recorded or not recorded. Data on individuals or organisations should not under any circumstances be collected or held solely on the basis that such a person or organisation supports unpopular causes or on the basis of race or creed.

17. It is also important to ensure that, wherever possible, information recorded about an individual is authenticated and does not give a false or misleading impression. Care should be taken to ensure that only necessary and relevant information is recorded and retained. Each Special Branch should therefore maintain an effective system both for updating information where necessary and for weeding out and destroying information which can no longer be clearly related to the discharge of its functions.

18. Access to information held by Special Branch should be strictly limited to those who have a particular need to know. Under no circumstances should information be passed to commercial firms or to employers' organisations.

19. The security of records maintained by Special Branch is of paramount importance. Because of the sensitivity of the information concerned and because of the damage to individuals which might result if unauthorised persons were to gain access to it, or if improper use were made of the information, Special Branches must ensure that the most stringent and appropriate precautions are taken to safeguard the information and to protect it against both unauthorised access or disclosure and accidental loss.

## Definitions

20. Espionage – Covert or illegal attempts to acquire information or materials in order to assist a foreign power.

- Sabotage – An act falling short of a military operation, or an omission, intended to cause physical damage in order to assist a hostile foreign power, or to further a subversive political aim.

- Terrorism – The use of violence for political ends, including any use of violence for the purpose of putting the public or any section of the public in fear.

- Subversion – Subversive activities are those which threaten the safety or well being of the State, and which are intended to undermine or overthrow parliamentary democracy by political, industrial or violent means.

Home Office
December 1984

# APPENDIX IV

## Extracts from the Annual Report of Canada's Security Intelligence Review Committee for 1987/8

Disbandment of the counter-subversion branch will stem overreaction to the rather modest threats Canada faces from home-grown radicals.

We believe that Parliament and the public expect the Security Intelligence Review Committee to have strong opinions and to state them clearly in its annual report.

Our mandate as a Committee is to see that CSIS carries out its work effectively, on the one hand, but without unreasonable or unnecessary intrusion on individual rights, on the other.

CSIS's job is to collect *intelligence* (their emphasis). Wiretap tapes commonly include a great deal of personal and other information that does not belong in secret files.

Oversight in one form or another is becoming the common experience of Western intelligence agencies.

The revised Operation Manual places a duty on investigators to ensure that the use of intrusive techniques is weighed against possible damage to constitutional rights and freedoms.

The Warrant Review Committee includes a Justice Department lawyer to act as 'devil's advocate', challenging the need for each warrant in the first place.

A proclivity for investigative techniques is endemic in CSIS; the Service seems to give more credibility to information it has ferreted out through investigation than to information available to any astute reader.

We can assure Canadians that we will continue to examine all warrants each year, and will immediately inform the Solicitor General and, if necessary, Parliament; should there be any misuse, in our opinion, of CSIS powers.

Making the service more representative of the society it serves is an important objective in recruitment. [The committee noted that ethnic minorities were under-represented in CSIS.]

Feeling that they [ethnic communities] are under the eye of the authorities, other members of these communities could be discouraged from exercising their rights of legitimate and lawful dissent. One scholarly study cites more than 100 definitions [of terrorism].

Today, membership in a group suspected of politically-motivated violence is not in itself sufficient grounds for targeting an individual in the first instance.

CSIS insistence on protecting their sources sometimes leaves the police wondering whether they are getting all the information they would like.

It is a common criticism in the security intelligence field throughout the Western world that governments do not give their intelligence agencies clear enough direction, and this appears to be true in Canada.

We have an ongoing tug-of-war with CSIS over the disclosure of information to complainants... We have a responsibility to ensure that complainants know enough to make an informed response to allegations that have been made against them... In both Australia and New Zealand we were told that disclosure is not a problem.

There is another need to know – the public's need to know what is being done in its name. Many details of security and intelligence work must, of course, remain secret for the obvious reasons: publicity would arm democracy's foes. But much can be told with out danger to security and it should be told.

[The report concludes with a diagram of Canada's security and intelligence apparatus and phone numbers of its secretariat, research and complaints officers.]

# APPENDIX V

## Making Complaints Against the Security Service

Leaflets entitled 'Complaints Against the Security Service', available to the general public, have been distributed by the Home Office to outlets including police stations, libraries and Citizens Advice Bureaux. People who want to make a complaint may request the Security Service Tribunal to investigate whether MI5 has acted against them or their property or given vetting information to their employer or prospective employer should apply to:

PO Box 18
London SE1 0TZ.

Complaints concerning interceptions of communications (whether by post or telephone conversations) should be addressed to the:

Interception of Communications Tribunal
PO Box 44
London SE1 0TX.

This was set up by the 1985 Interception of Communications Act.

# NOTES

## INTRODUCTION

1. *The Independent*, 3 December 1986.
2. A phrase used throughout the Commons debates on the Security Service Bill in the autumn and winter of 1988/89.
3. *The Listener*, 12 August 1982.
4. *The Observer*, 12 May 1984.

## CHAPTER ONE: Induction to a Closed World

1. Peter Wright, *Spycatcher* (1987, New York). The book was published in Australia the following year after lengthy and expensive litigation in which the British Government failed to suppress it. The Government also failed in the English courts to prevent the press here from reporting the contents of *Spycatcher*. Under the present state of the law, the book can be distributed, but not published, in Britain. Margaret Thatcher's statement was quoted in *The Guardian*, 27 January 1988.
2. Clive Ponting, *The Right to Know* (1985), p. 184. Richard Norton-Taylor, *The Ponting Affair* (1985), p. 110.
3. Letter from Mrs Thatcher to Richard Shepherd MP, 3 February 1988.
4. See Appendix III.
5. *Hansard*, 2 March 1978, col. 650.
6. See Phillip Knightley, *The Second Oldest Profession* (1986).
7. A V Dicey, *An Introduction to the Study of the Constitution*, 10th edition (1959).
8. *Lord Denning's Report*, Cmnd. 2152 (September 1963).
9. Wright, *Op.cit.*, p. 54.
10. *Ibid.*, p. 31.
11. Court of Appeal, 22 January 1988.
12. *Ibid.*
13. *Ibid.*
14. Court of Appeal, 10 February 1988.
15. Security Service Act 1989, Section 3.
16. Interception of Communications Act 1985, Section 4.
17. Wright, *Op. cit.*, p. 353.
18. Code for Crown Prosecutors (HMSO 1986).
19. *Hansard*, 29 January 1951, col. 681.
20. *Hansard*, 25 January 1989, col. 21.
21. Court of Appeal, 29 March 1977.
22. House of Lords Judicial Committee (Law Lords), 22 November 1984.

23. *Ibid.*
24. Duncan Campbell, *Phonetappers and the Security State* (1981), p. 40.
25. *Hansard*, 5 December 1988, col. 52.
26. *The Independent on Sunday*, 25 February 1990.
27. The Zircon eavesdropping satellite is believed to have been put into orbit by a US Titan rocket in late 1989 or early 1990.
28. *Hansard*, 24 October 1988, col. 17.
29. See ministerial comments throughout the debates on the Security Service and Offical Secrets Acts, winter/spring 1988/89.
30. Letter to Dale Campbell-Savours MP from Donald Limon, 21 July 1987.
31. *Treatise on the Law, Privileges, Proceedings and Usage of Parliament* (20th ed.), p. 342.
32. Harold Wilson, *The Governance of Britain* (1977), p. 167.
33. *Ibid.*

## CHAPTER TWO: OFFICIAL SECRETS

1. In the summer of 1989, Thatcher said that the manuscripts had been sent to HMSO, the government publishers, for publication in 1990. *The History of Strategic Deception in the Second World War* by Sir Michael Howard, former Regius Professor of History at Oxford University, included an account of how enemy agents captured in Britain collaborated with MI5 by sending back misleading information to Germany. A book by Anthony Simkins, a former MI5 deputy director-general, concentrates on the wartime activities of the Security Service and the Special Operations Executive (SOE).
2. The book has been published in three editions – in 1974, 1980, and 1983 – the latter two the result of the disclosure of material previously classified.
3. The D Notice system was set up in 1912, a year after the Official Secrets Act of 1911. It is administered by the Defence, Press and Broadcasting Committee (the D Notice Committee), a body consisting of senior Whitehall officials from the Ministry of Defence, the Home Office and the Foreign Office, and a number of senior executives from media organisations. Its secretary is a recently retired senior armed forces officer – currently Rear Admiral Higgins – with an office in the MoD. He can be contacted by editors and journalists if they want advice about whether information they may publish contravenes D Notices. These include the position of nuclear submarines and the activities of the security services. The D Notice system has no legal

standing and is increasingly ignored, editors preferring to make their own judgments, or seeking the advice of their own lawyers.

4. Notably Chapman Pincher, *Their Trade is Treachery* (1981), and Nigel West, *Molehunt* (1987).
5. Anthony Cavendish, *Inside Intelligence* (1987).
6. Chapman Pincher, *Traitors: The Labyrinth of Treason* (1987).
7. *The Guardian*, 22 February 1989.
8. Andrew Boyle, *The Climate of Treason: Five who Spied for Russia* (1979).
9. *Intelligence and National Security*, Vol. 1, No. 1 (1985).
10. *The Guardian*, 15 October 1985.
11. Letter to *The Guardian*, 29 November 1985.
12. For an entertaining account of Mackenzie's secrets trial, see David Hooper, *Official Secrets* (1987), Chapter 3.
13. *Hansard*, 25 January 1989, col. 1096.
14. *Ibid.*
15. The Westland affair led to the resignation of Michael Heseltine, the Defence Secretary, and Leon Brittan, the Trade and Industry Secretary. The role in the affair of Charles Powell and Bernard Ingham, two of the Prime Minister's closest advisers, remains unclear. Mrs Thatcher has denied that she was involved in the decision to leak part of a letter from Sir Patrick Mayhew, the Solicitor-General, though she is reported to have told her advisers, before a crucial Commons debate, that she might not still be Prime Minister by six o'clock that evening. For an account of the Westland affair, see Tam Dalyell, *Misrule* (1987).
16. Mark Hollingsworth and Charles Tremayne, *The Economic League: The Silent McCarthyism* (1989).
17. Christopher Andrew, *Secret Service* (1985), pp. 339-40.
18. For an account of the ABC case, see Crispin Aubrey, *Who's Watching You?* (1981).
19. Private interview.
20. *Tracts Beyond The Times*, Social Affairs Unit (1983).
21. A copy of *British Briefing*, marked 'Issue No. 12 1989' was sent, anonymously, to the author.
22. Josef Frolik, *The Frolik Defection* (1975).
23. The Maxwell-Fyfe Directive was first published in the Denning Report on the Profumo affair.
24. *Hansard*, 23 January 1989, col. 767.
25. Evidence to the Commons Treasury and Civil Service Committee, 12 February 1986.
26. *Hansard*, 21 November 1979, col. 402.

27. Boyle, *Op.cit.*
28. *Hansard*, 11 December 1979, col. 1091.
29. New South Wales Supreme Court, Sydney, Australia, 13 March 1987.
30. Oral statement, House of Commons, 26 March 1981.
31. Evidence at the trial, Heinemann, Australia and Peter Wright against HM Attorney-General, New South Wales Supreme Court, November/December 1986.
32. *Ibid.*
33. *Ibid.*
34. Kane's book has still not been published.
35. Cmnd. 9514 (1985).
36. *The Guardian*, 21 April 1989.
37. The High Court, 21 December 1987.
38. *Hansard* (House of Lords), 18 April 1989, col. 717.

## CHAPTER THREE: How Targets are Defined

1. Home Affairs Committee, Session 1984-85, Special Branch, *Minutes of Evidence*, 16 January 1985, p. 52.
2. *Ibid.*, p. 56.
3. 'Panorama', BBC Television, 2 March 1981.
4. *New Society*, 31 May 1984. Miranda Ingram, a former MI5 officer, was writing at the time Michael Bettaney, another young MI5 officer, was arrested after trying to offer secrets to the Soviet Embassy in London. Bettaney's arrest sparked off a public debate in some sections of the media and among some MPs about the activities and, above all, the management of MI5.
5. *Hansard*, 15 January 1988, col. 612.
6. *Hansard*, 3 December 1986, col. 959.
7. *The Observer*, 28 February 1982.
8. Letter from Leon Brittan to John Prescott, 25 January 1985.
9. *Hansard*, 15 December 1988, col. 1114.
10. Recommendation No. R(87)15 of the Committee of Ministers to Member States Regulating the Use of Personal Data in the Public Sector, Council of Europe, 1987.
11. *Ibid.*
12. Address to the Ditchley Foundation Conference, 7-9 October 1988, on 'The Oversight of and the Limits on Intelligence Work in a Democracy'.
13. *Ibid.*
14. *Ibid.*, A Note to the Director.
15. *Hansard*, 17 January 1989, col. 222.

16. Sir Ian Gilmour, Richard Shepherd, Jonathan Aitken and Robert McLennan were among the MPs who proposed the amendment.
17. *Hansard*, 25 January 1988, col. 7.
18. Meeting between Mrs Thatcher and Civil Service union leaders at 10 Downing Street on 23 February 1984.
19. Security Service Act 1989, Section 1(2).
20. Interception of Communications Act 1985, Report of the Commissioner for 1988, Cmnd. 652 (1989).
21. The Interception of Communications in the United Kingdom, Cmnd. 9438 (1985).
22. On vetting in general, see Ian Linn, *Application Refused: Employment Vetting by the State* (The Civil Liberties Trust, 1990) and Mark Hollingsworth and Richard Norton-Taylor, *Blacklist* (1988).
23. Cmnd. 9715 (1956).
24. Harry Houghton and his fiancée, Ethel Gee, passed information about the Admiralty Underwater Weapons Establishment in Portland to the Soviet spies Gordon Lonsdale (Konon Molody) and to Helen and Peter Kroger.
25. Blake was sentenced to a record gaol sentence of 42 years after a largely secret trial in 1961. Claims, notably by Chapman Pincher, that the sentence reflected the number of British agents he betrayed have been described by his defence counsel, Lord Hutchinson QC, as 'absolute rubbish'. Blake escaped from Wormwood Scrubs in 1966. See Michael Randle and Pat Pottle, *The Blake Escape* (1989).
26. Cmnd. 1681 (1962).
27. *Ibid.*
28. The allegation was perpetrated by a group of MI5 officers, notably Peter Wright. It has been generally discounted.
29. Cmnd. 8540, pp. 3 and 4.
30. Written parliamentary answer, 3 April 1985.
31. *Ibid.*
32. *Hansard* (House of Lords) 26 February 1975, col. 947.

## CHAPTER FOUR: The Security Services Network

1. Denning, *Op.cit.*, p. 79.
2. *Ibid.*
3. *Ibid.*, p. 80.
4. *Ibid.*
5. The Franks Committee on Section 2 of the Official Secrets Act 1911, Cmnd. 5104 (1972), Vol. 3, p. 243.
6. Denning, *Op.cit.*, p. 80.

7. *Hansard*, 16 December 1963, col. 857.
8. Wilson, *Op.cit.*, p. 167.
9. BBC Radio 4, 'My Country Right or Wrong', 29 May 1988.
10. In August 1984 the European Court of Human Rights found Britain in breach of Article 8 of the European Rights Convention (guaranteeing the right to respect for private and family life, an individual's home and correspondence). The case was brought by James Malone, a Dorking antiques dealer acquitted in 1977 of receiving stolen goods. It was made clear in police evidence during his trial that his telephone had been tapped.
11. *New Society*, 31 May 1984.
12. David Leigh, *The Wilson Plot* (1988).
13. Steve Uglow, *Policing Liberal Society* (1988), p. 143.
14. Home Affairs Committee, Session 1984-85, *Op.cit.*
15. *Hansard*, 7 March 1988, col. 73.
16. *The Observer*, 10 January 1982.
17. Home Affairs Committee, *Op.cit.*, and quoted in 'Big Brother's Invisible Men', *The Guardian*, 15 June 1985.
18. BBC Radio, 'File on Four', 10 August 1982.
19. Home Affairs Committee, *Op.cit.*
20. *The Observer*, 31 January 1982.
21. See Appendix III.
22. Personal interview.
23. *Hansard*, 11 July 1988, col. 75.
24. Ken Flower, *Serving Secretly* (1987), Chapter 5.
25. Nigel West, *The Friends* (1988).
26. Aubrey, *Op.cit.*
27. Meeting at 10 Downing Street, 23 February 1984.
28. Letter from Dennis Mitchell to David Steel MP, John Smith MP, Terence Higgins MP and the Bishop of Gloucester, 27 January 1987.
29. *The Guardian*, 9 May 1986.
30. See Jeffrey Richardson and Desmond Ball, *The Ties that Bind* (1985), pp. 42 and 173.
31. *New York Times*, 24 July 1986.
32. Gordon Winter, *Inside Boss, South Africa's Secret Police* (1981).
33. James Bamford, *The Puzzle Palace* (1983), p. 253.

## CHAPTER FIVE: How The Security Network Links Up

1. The leak of documents, apparently from the BSSO, gave the IRA a propaganda coup in 1989. See *New Statesman and Society*, 20 October 1989.

2. *Hansard*, 19 May 1988, col. 1095.
3. *The Observer*, 3 January 1988.
4. *Ibid.*
5. Private information.
6. Wright, *Op.cit.*, p. 360.
7. See Duncan Campbell and Steve Connor, *On the Record: Surveillance, Computers and Privacy* (1986), Chapter 4.
8. *Ibid.*, p. 36.
9. *Ibid.*, p. 191.
10. *Ibid.*, p. 250.
11. Report of the Data Protection Committee, Cmnd. 7341 (1978), p. 220. The Lindop Committee distinguished between 'information' and 'intelligence'. Information, it said, was factual data, such as name and date of birth; in contrast, criminal intelligence may be speculation and hearsay. See also Campbell and Connor, *Op.cit.*, p. 218.
12. Personal interview.
13. *The Guardian*, 16 February 1990.
14. Philip Knightley and Caroline Kennedy, *An Affair of State* (1987).
15. For an account of the Littlejohn affair, see Jonathan Bloch and Patrick Fitzgerald, *British Intelligence and Covert Action* (1983), pp. 217-225.
16. Bill Graham, *Break-in* (1987).
17. *The Observer*, 2 April 1989, and Yorkshire Television, 'First Tuesday', 4 April 1989.
18. *The Observer*, 7 August 1988.
19. *Handbook of Security*, a privately published handbook for private sector security firms, Kluwer Publishing Limited (periodically updated).
20. Yorkshire Television, 'First Tuesday', 4 April 1989.
21. Hollingsworth and Norton-Taylor, *Op.cit.*, p. 189.
22. Evidence supplied to the author.
23. Granada Television, 'World in Action', 8 February 1988.
24. Personal interview.
25. Granada Television, 'World in Action', 1 February 1988.
26. *New York Times*, 25 February 1967.
27. Private interview.
28. See, for example, *New Statesman and Society*, 20 October 1989.
29. Private information.

## CHAPTER SIX: Security and Intelligence Operations

1. *The Observer*, 30 October 1988.
2. *Police Review*, 15 February 1985.

3. Interception of Communications Act, Report of the Commissioner for 1988, *Op.cit.*
4. Report of the Commissioner for 1986 (1987).
5. Private information.
6. Private information.
7. Patrick Fitzgerald and Mark Leopold, *Stranger on the Line: The Secret History of Phone Tapping* (1987).
8. See House of Commons Notices of Motions, Dale Campbell-Savours, 970, Telephone Tapping, 11 May 1987.
9. James Rusbridger, *The Intelligence Game* (1989), p. 165, and Campbell and Conner, *Op.cit.*, p. 205.
10. *New Statesman*, 19 November 1982.
11. *The Independent*, 3 December 1986.
12. 'MI5's Official Secrets', Channel 4, 20/20 Vision, 8 March 1985.
13. *Ibid.*
14. *Ibid.*
15. *The Observer*, 10 March 1985.
16. Evidence to the House of Commons Home Affairs Committee, 16 January 1985.
17. 20/20 Vision, *Op.cit.*
18. *Ibid.*
19. Hollingsworth and Norton-Taylor, *Op.cit.*, p. 139.
20. 20/20 Vision, *Op.cit.*
21. Barbara Castle, *The Castle Diaries 1964-70* (1978).
22. Hollingsworth and Norton-Taylor, *Op.cit.*, p. 123.
23. 20/20 Vision, *Op.cit.*
24. *Ibid.*
25. Hollingsworth and Norton-Taylor, *Op.cit.*, p. 1.
26. 20/20 Vision, *Op.cit.*
27. *Ibid.*
28. See Hollingsworth and Norton-Taylor, *Op.cit.*, p. 135.
29. *Ibid.*
30. Letter from Sir Vernon Kell to US embassy in London, 5 March 1937.
31. *The Economist*, 6 March 1982.
32. 20/20 Vision, *Op.cit.*
33. Private information.
34. 20/20 Vision, *Op.cit.*
35. Private information.
36. *Hansard*, 23 January 1989, col. 767.
37. Agee, a former CIA Officer, was deported along with Mark Hosenball; see Aubrey, *Op.cit.*

38. *The Guardian*, 19 April 1984.
39. *Hansard*, 17 January 1989, col. 180.
40. *Hansard*, 25 January 1989, col. 1082.
41. *Hansard*, 25 January 1989, col. 1051.
42. Fred Holroyd, *War Without Honour* (1989).
43. *The Sunday Times*, 22 March 1987.
44. Anthony Verrier, *Through the Looking Glass*, (1983).
45. Private information.
46. See *The Sunday Times*, 2 April 1989.
47. *The Gibraltar Report*, Hilary Kitchin (NCCL), 1989.
48. Interview with the author.
49. Letter seen by the author. See also Paul Foot, *Who Framed Colin Wallace?* (1989).
50. *Hansard*, 30 January 1990, col. 90.
51. David Leigh, *The Wilson Plot* (1988), especially p. 109.
52. Wright, *Op.cit.*, p. 369.
53. Leigh, *Op.cit.*, p. 113 ff.
54. See Barrie Penrose and Roger Courtiour, *The Pencourt File* (1978).
55. *Hansard*, 6 May 1987, col. 726.
56. Evidence exhibited to New South Wales Supreme Court, Sydney, November 1986.
57. *Hansard*, 6 May 1987, col. 726.
58. Both Merlyn Rees and Lord Callaghan repeated this view in Parliament and in the media during the debates on the Security Services Bill in 1988 and 1989.
59. Personal interview.
60. BBC Radio 4, 'The Profession of Intelligence', 10 February 1982.
61. Wright, *Op.cit.*, Chapter 6.
62. *Ibid.*, p. 160.
63. Bloch and Fitzgerald, *Op.cit.*, p. 137.
64. Bob Woodward, *Veil* (1987), p. 72.
65. The Government has consistently refused to comment on this. See, for example, Alan Clark, the junior defence minister's answer to Tam Dalyell MP, *Hansard*, 8 July 1987, col. 347.
66. *The Independent*, 27 October 1986.


## CHAPTER SEVEN: How Others Do It


1. *The Independent*, 10 March 1988.
2. *The Independent*, 10 May 1989.
3. *The Guardian*, 12 July 1988.
4. *The Financial Times*, 3 August 1988.

5. *Ibid.*
6. *Le Monde*, Paris, 31 January 1990.
7. *Leander v. Sweden*, European Court of Human Rights, Series A No. 116, 26 March 1987, App. No. 9248/81.
8. *Klass and Others v. Federal Republic of Germany*, European Court of Human Rights, Series A No. 28, 6 September 1978.
9. *Ibid.*
10. Stansfield Turner, *Secrecy and Democracy* (1986), p. 145.
11. *Ibid.*, p. 195 ff.
12. *Ibid.*, p. 145.
13. *Ibid.*, p. 142.
14. Speech to Kansas Law School, November 1976. Mondale was a member of the Church Committee.
15. 99th Congress 1st Session, Compilation of Intelligence Laws and related laws and the executive orders of interest to the National Intelligence Communities, Government Printing Office, July 1985.
16. *Ibid.*
17. Personal interviews.
18. Penn Kimball, *The File* (1984).
19. *Ibid.*
20. Data Protection Act 1984. See Hollingsworth and Norton-Taylor, *Op.cit.*, p. 228.
21. Freedom and Security Under the Law, the second Report of the Commission of Inquiry Concerning Certain Activities of the Royal Canadian Mounted Police (1981).
22. *Ibid.*, pp. 513-514.
23. The Canadian Security Intelligence Service Act 1984, Section 21.
24. *Ibid.*, Section 2(d).
25. See, for example, Security Intelligence Review Committee, *Annual Report 1987-1988*, p. 8.
26. The Canadian Security Intelligence Service Act, Section 39(2).
27. *Ibid.*, Section 41(1).
28. *Ibid.*
29. *Ibid.*, Sections 70, 73 and 89.
30. Security Intelligence Review Committee, *Annual Report 1986-1987*, p. 5.
31. *Ibid.*, p. 33.
32. *Ibid.*, p. 39.
33. Security Intelligence Review Committee, *Annual Report 1987-1988*, p. 13.
34. Harvey Barnett, *Tale of the Scorpion* (Australia, 1988), p. 13.
35. *Ibid.*, p. 213.

36. The Inspector-General of Intelligence and Security Act (1986), Section 2(a).
37. Australian Security Intelligence Organisation, *Report to the Parliament 1986-87*, p. 4.
38. *Ibid.*, p. 14.
39. Turner, *Op.cit.*, p. xvii.

## CHAPTER EIGHT: The Case for Accountability

1. *New Society*, 31 May 1984.
2. *The Observer*, 12 May 1985.
3. *New Statesman*, 5 December 1986.
4. *The Independent*, Magazine, 20 January 1990.
5. Turner, *Op.cit.*, p. 151.
6. 20/20 Vision, *Op.cit.*
7. Falkland Islands Review, Report of a Committee of Privy Counsellors, Cmnd. 8787 (1983).
8. *Ibid.*, p. 85.
9. *Hansard*, 17 January 1989, col. 289.
10. *Hansard*, 17 January 1989, col. 251.
11. 'My Country Right or Wrong'.
12. Turner, *Op.cit.*, p. 150.
13. Barnett, *Op.cit.*, p. 4.
14. *Ibid.*, p. 4.
15. Turner, *Op.cit.*, p. 150.
16. Ditchley Conference Report No. D88/11, 1988.
17. *Ibid.*
18. Turner, *Op.cit.*, p. 149.
19. Judgment, New South Wales Supreme Court, March 1987.
20. The High Court, 21 December 1987.
21. Sir Percy Sillitoe, *Cloak Without Dagger* (1955), p. 181.
22. Leander and Klass cases.

## APPENDIX II

1. *Hansard* (House of Lords), 20 April 1989, col. 877.
2. *Hansard* (House of Lords), 27 February 1989, col. 864.

## Civil Liberties Trust Publications

**General** (Please add 70p per title p & p, orders over £10.00 post free)

| | |
|---|---|
| *The Price of Justice*: Howard Levenson | £ 2.95 |
| *Drifting into a Law and Order Society:* Stuart Hall | £ 0.95 |
| *Right of Silence*: James Wood and Adam Crawford | £ 2.95 |
| *In Defence of the Realm? The Case for Accountable Security Services:* Richard Norton-Taylor | £ 3.95 |
| *Application Refused: Employment Vetting by the State*: Ian Linn | £ 3.95 |

**Policing and Criminal Procedure**

| | |
|---|---|
| *Troops in Strikes*: Steve Peak | £ 4.95 |
| *Police Authorities During the Miners' Strike*: Sarah Spencer | £ 1.95 |
| *Policing the Miners' Strike*: edited Bob Fine & Robert Millar | £ 4.95 |
| *Controlling the Constable*: Tony Jefferson & Richard Grimshaw | £ 7.95 |

**Northern Ireland**

| | |
|---|---|
| *Supergrasses*: Tony Gifford QC | £ 1.50 |
| *Abolishing the Diplock Courts*: S C Greer & A White | £ 3.95 |
| *Incitement to Disaffection*: Thom Young | £ 1.20 |

**Race, Nationality and Immigration**

| | |
|---|---|
| *Immigration, Law and Practice*: Lawrence Grant & Ian Martin | £18.00 |
| *Immigration, Law and Practice (First Supplement)*: Lawrence Grant & Ian Martin | £10.25 |
| *Towards a Just Immigration Policy*: edited Anne Dummett | £ 7.95 |
| *Black Magistrates*: Michael King & Colin May | £ 4.95 |

**Ethnic Minority Language Leaflets**:

*Making a Complaint Against the Police* £1.00 per set (inc. p&p)
(individual copies free with an SAE, bulk rates available on request)

Gujerati
Hindi
Bengali
Chinese
Spanish
Urdu
Punjabi

**Women's Rights**

| | |
|---|---|
| *Judging Inequality*: Alice Leonard | £ 9.95 |
| *Women Inside*: Silvia Casale | £ 6.95 |

# Liberty Publications

**Civil Liberty Briefings**

(all priced at £1.00 inclusive of p&p)

Police & Criminal Evidence Act
Police Accountability
The Conservative Government's Record on Civil Liberties
Travellers on the Road
Public Order Act
The Privacy Implications of the Poll Tax
Your Right to See Your File
The Employment Bill 1987
The Official Secrets Act
The UK Record on Civil Liberties
Identity Cards and the Threat to Civil Liberties
A Bill of Rights
Freedom of Expression in the UK
Employment and Trade Union Legislation in the 1980s
Who's Watching You? Video Surveillance in Public Places
Prisoners' Rights
Report on the Security Service Bill
Background Paper on Pornography and Censorship

**General**

(Please add 70p per title to cover p&p; orders of £10 and over, post free)

| | |
|---|---|
| *We Protest – The Public Order Debate*: Peter Thornton | £ 3.95 |
| *Trade Unionists & Public Order*: Marie Staunton | £ 1.50 |
| *Free to Walk Together*: Marie Staunton | £ 1.50 |
| *Changing Contempt of Court*: Andrew Nicol & Heather Rogers | £ 1.20 |
| *The National Council for Civil Liberties – The First 50 Years*: Mark Lilly | £ 5.95 |
| *The Purging of the Civil Service*: NCCL | £ 0.95 |
| *Civil Rights for Civil Servants*: NCCL | £ 0.95 |
| *Public Order Law*: Peter Thornton | £11.95 |
| *Stonehenge*: NCCL | £ 1.95 |
| *Fire Under the Carpet – Civil Liberties in the 1930s*: Sylvia Scaffardi | £ 4.95 |
| *Gay Workers, Trade Unions & The Law*: Chris Beer, Roland Jeffery & Terry Munyard | £ 1.75 |
| *Section 28: A Practical Guide to the Law & its Implications*: Madeleine Colvin | £ 4.50 |
| *Decade of Decline: Civil Liberties in the Thatcher Years*: Peter Thornton | £ 3.95 |
| *Penguin/Liberty Guide to Your Rights*: Malcolm Hurwitt & Peter Thornton | £ 4.99 |
| *The Economic League: The Silent McCarthyism:* Mark Hollingsworth & Charles Tremayne | £ 3.95 |

**Policing And Criminal Procedure**

*Called to Account – The Case for Police Accountability in England & Wales*: Sarah Spencer: £ 3.95
*Civil Liberties in the Miners' Dispute* (Independent Enquiry Report) £ 1.50
*Poor Law*: Ros Franey £ 1.95
*A Fair Cop*: Patricia Hewitt £ 1.75
*Southall – 23 April 1979* (Independent Enquiry Report) £ 2.20
*Death of Blair Peach* (Independent Enquiry Report) £ 1.50
*Operation Fire/Operation Tan* £ 1.25
*No Way in Wapping* £ 1.95

**Northern Ireland**

*Strip Searching – Women Remand Prisoners at Armagh Prison 1982-1985*: NCCL Report £ 1.95
*The New Prevention of Terrorism Act 1984*: Catherine Scorer, Sarah Spencer & Patricia Hewitt £ 2.50
*The Gibraltar Report – Independent Observer's Report on the Gibraltar Enquiry:* Hilary Kitchin £ 4.00
*Enduring Inequality: Religious Discrimination in Employment in Northern Ireland*: Vincent McCormack & Joe O'Hara £ 3.95

**Privacy**

*Whose File is it Anyway?* Ruth Cohen £ 0.20
*Data Protection*: Roger Cornwell & Marie Staunton £ 3.95
*The Zircon Affair*: Peter Thornton £ 0.95
Privacy and the Poll Tax: Liberty / ALA
*Public Information Leaflet* £ 1.00
*A Guide to Good Practice for Councillors* £ 2.50
*A Guide to Good Practice for Local Government Officers* £ 5.50

**Womens' Rights**

*Positive Action for Women*: Paddy Stamp & Sadie Robarts £ 4.95
*Judging Women*: Polly Pattullo £ 0.95
*No More Peanuts*: Jo Morris £ 2.50
*Amending the Equality Laws*: Catherine Scorer & Ann Sedley £ 0.95
*The Rape Controversy*: Melissa Benn, Anna Coote & Tess Gill £ 1.50
*Sexual Harassment at Work*: Ann Sedley & Melissa Benn £ 0.95
*Maternity Rights at Work*: Jean Coussins, Lyn Durward & Ruth Evans £ 1.50
*Women Won't Benefit*:: Hilary Land & Sue Ward £ 1.95
*The Shiftwork Swindle*: Jean Coussins £ 0.60
*The Equality Report*: Jean Coussins £ 1.20
*The Unequal Breadwinner*: Ruth Lister & Les Wilson £ 0.35

**Race, Nationality and Immigration**

*Race Relations Rights*: Paul Gordon, John Wright & Patricia Hewitt £ 1.95
*British Nationality*: Ann Dummett & Ian Martin £ 2.95

# THE CIVIL LIBERTIES TRUST

The Civil Liberties Trust, the sister organisation to the National Council for Civil Liberties (*Liberty*), is a registered charity which was established in 1963 to undertake research and education on civil liberty issues.

## *How You Can Help*

The Civil Liberties Trust depends on generous public support for its survival. As a registered charity, the Trust can recover tax from the Inland Revenue on any covenanted donation.

- ☐ I enclose a donation to the Civil Liberties Trust
- ☐ I would like to make a covenant to the Civil Liberties Trust (form overleaf)
- ☐ Please send me information about the work of the Trust
- ☐ Please send me information about joining Liberty

**Make a covenant to the Civil Liberties Trust and bring us the one-third you pay in tax.**

If you pay tax, there's a simple way of increasing the value of your gift at no extra cost to yourself. If you fill in the form overleaf, we can claim back the tax you have paid, increasing your donation by one-third if you pay tax at the basic rate.

# Covenant Form

My name is . . . . . . . . . . . . . . . . . . . . . . . . . . . . .

and my address is . . . . . . . . . . . . . . . . . . . . . . . . . .

. . . . . . . . . . . . . . . . . . . . . . . . . . . . . . . . . . .

. . . . . . . . . . . . . . . . . . . . . . . . . . . . . . . . . . .

. . . . . . . . . . . . . . . . . . . . . . . . . . . . . . . . . . .

I promise to pay the Civil Liberties Trust £.........every year/half-year/quarter*. My covenant will last for 4 years/7 years*(but will be cancelled if I die sooner). *Delivered under my hand and seal*

Signature . . . . . . . . . . . . . . . . . . . . . . . . . . . . . .

on . . . . . . . . . . (date).

*Please get a friend to witness your signature:*

My witness's signature . . . . . . . . . . . . . . . . . . . . . .

*Now please fill in the Banker's Order Form*

Date . . . . . . . . To . . . . . . . . . . . . . . . . . . . . . . .

. . . . . . . . . . . . . . . . . . . . . . . . . . . . . . . . . . .

. . . . . . . . . . . . . . . . . . . . . . . . . . . . . . . . . . .

(Bank name and branch address)

Please pay to the credit of the Charities Aid Foundation (D) account number 36880043 at NatWest Bank Ltd, 126 High Holborn, London WC1 (sort code 60-30-06) for the later credit of The Civil Liberties Trust on...................... (date) the sum of £........... and the same sum on the same date annually/half yearly/quarterly* until 19........ (last year of payment). Please debit my account number.............. accordingly.

Signature . . . . . . . . . . . . . . . . . . . . . . . . . . . . . .

Name . . . . . . . . . . . . . . . . . . . . . . . . . . . . . . . . .

Address . . . . . . . . . . . . . . . . . . . . . . . . . . . . . . .

. . . . . . . . . . . . . . . . . . . . . . . . . . . . . . . . . . .

**delete whichever does not apply.*